Copilot: The Workplace AI Guide

Practical AI for Microsoft 365

Ken Tannenbaum

2026

Finnoybu Press

Copilot: The Workplace AI Guide

2026 Edition

Practical AI for Microsoft 365

Published by Finnoybu Press

For permissions and inquiries: press@finnoybu.org

First Edition: 2026

About the Author

Ken Tannenbaum is a technologist, entrepreneur, and AI governance researcher. He is the founder of Finnoybu Press and the founder/steward of the AEGIS Initiative, an open framework for AI safety and accountability. Learn more at aegis-initiative.com.

When he's not building governance standards for artificial intelligence, he's helping everyday people understand and use it.

Dedication

To every worker who has ever wished their computer would just do the thing already — your day has come.

And to Microsoft, for finally making Clippy's dream a reality. He would be so proud.

The AI for Everyone Series

This book is part of the **AI for Everyone** series by Finnoybu Press, designed to help real people use AI tools effectively. Visit **press.finnoybu.org** for the latest titles and updates.

Collection One: Product Deep Dives

- *ChatGPT: The Definitive Guide (2026 Edition)*
- *ChatGPT: The Power User Guide (2026 Edition)*
- *Claude: The Definitive Guide (2026 Edition)*
- *Claude Code: The Power User Guide (2026 Edition)*
- *Gemini: The Complete Guide (2026 Edition)*
- *Gemini: The Advanced Guide (2026 Edition)*
- *Copilot: The Workplace AI Guide (2026 Edition)*
- *Copilot: The Advanced Workplace Guide (2026 Edition)*
- *Perplexity: The Research Playbook (2026 Edition)*
- *Perplexity: The Advanced Research Playbook (2026 Edition)*

Collection Two: Product Guides

- *NotebookLM: From Sources to Audio Overviews (2026 Edition)*
- *DeepSeek: Code, Math, and Reasoning (2026 Edition)*
- *Cursor: The AI Code Editor (2026 Edition)*
- *OpenClaw: Agentic AI for Everyday Work (2026 Edition)*

Collection Three: Cross-Platform Skills

- *AI Systems Playbook (2026 Edition)*
- *AI Prompt Engineering (2026 Edition)*
- *AI for Developers (2026 Edition)*
- *AI for Business (2026 Edition)*
- *AI for Students (2026 Edition)*
- *AI Governance for Practitioners (2026 Edition)*
- *Securing Agentic AI (2026 Edition)*

Table of Contents

Introduction 11

Part I: Getting Started 15

Chapter 1: What Is Microsoft Copilot? 17

Chapter 2: Choosing the Right Plan 23

Chapter 3: Setting Up Your Account 31

Chapter 4: Understanding Copilot's Models and Modes 39

Chapter 5: Your First Conversations 47

Part II: Everyday Use 55

Chapter 6: Writing with Copilot 57

Chapter 7: Research and Learning 65

Chapter 8: Everyday Productivity 75

Part III: Copilot at Work 83

Chapter 9: Work and Professional Use 85

Chapter 10: Copilot in Word 93

Chapter 11: Copilot in Excel 103

Chapter 12: Copilot in PowerPoint 113

Chapter 13: Copilot in Outlook 123

Chapter 14: Copilot in Teams 133

Part IV: Advanced Features 143

Chapter 15: Image Generation with Designer 145

Chapter 16: Copilot Pages and Notebooks 155
Chapter 17: Think Deeper — Extended Reasoning 165
Chapter 18: Copilot Vision 173

Part V: Prompting and Technique 183

Chapter 19: Prompting Fundamentals 185
Chapter 20: Working with Long and Complex Tasks 195
Chapter 21: Output Formatting and Control 205

Part VI: Copilot for Every Audience 215

Chapter 22: Copilot for Students and Educators 217
Chapter 23: Copilot for Business and Teams 225
Chapter 24: Copilot for Developers 235

Part VII: Using AI Responsibly 245

Chapter 25: What Copilot Gets Wrong 247
Chapter 26: Privacy, Security, and Safe Use 255
Chapter 27: The Ethics of AI Assistance 263
Chapter 28: Epilogue — Where We Go from Here 271
Appendix A: Keyboard Shortcuts and Interface Tips 273
Appendix B: Prompt Template Library 277
Appendix C: Troubleshooting Common Issues 293
Appendix D: Glossary of AI Terms 299
Appendix E: What's New in 2025-2026 305
Appendix F: Resources and Further Reading 311

Introduction

What This Book Covers

Microsoft Copilot is one of the most ambitious AI products ever shipped. It is embedded in Windows, Edge, Microsoft 365, Teams, GitHub, and a standalone app you can use right now for free. It can write your emails, analyze your spreadsheets, build your presentations, generate images, search the web, summarize meetings, and hold a conversation about nearly anything.

The problem is not whether Copilot can help you. The problem is that nobody has explained — clearly, practically, and without marketing fluff — how to use it well.

That is what this book does.

We start at the beginning: what Copilot is, which plan is right for you, and how to set it up. Then we work through everyday use cases — writing, research, productivity, and personal tasks — before diving into Copilot inside each Microsoft 365 app: Word, Excel, PowerPoint, Outlook, and Teams. From there, we cover advanced features like image generation with Designer, Pages and Notebooks, Think Deeper mode, and Copilot Vision. We close with prompting techniques that make everything work better, specialized chapters for students, businesses, and developers, and a clear-eyed look at what Copilot gets wrong, how to stay safe, and how to use AI responsibly.

Who This Book Is For

This book is for anyone who uses — or is thinking about using — Microsoft Copilot. You do not need a technical background. You do not need to understand how AI works under the hood. You need to want to get more done with less effort, and to appreciate a guide that respects your time and intelligence.

If you are a student, a teacher, a manager, an accountant, a marketer, a writer, a small business owner, or someone who wants to understand what the fuss is about — this book is for you.

If you are already an experienced Copilot user looking for advanced techniques, enterprise deployment strategies, and developer workflows, the companion volume *Copilot: The Advanced Workplace Guide* picks up where this book leaves off.

How to Read This Book

You have two options. The first is to read it straight through. The chapters build on each other, and by the end you will have a thorough understanding of Copilot and a solid set of skills.

The second is to jump to whatever you need right now. Each chapter stands on its own. If you want to learn Copilot in Excel, go straight to Chapter 11. If you want better prompts, start at Chapter 19. The table of contents and appendices help you find what you need quickly.

Either approach works. This book will meet you where you are.

A Note on AI Assistance

This book was written with the assistance of AI tools. The full disclosure is in the front matter, but the short version: AI helped with research, drafting, and review. Every word was reviewed, edited, and approved by a human author. The prompts and examples come from hands-on testing. When I say something works, I have tried it myself.

A Note About Accuracy

Microsoft Copilot changes constantly. Microsoft ships updates regularly, sometimes weekly. Features get added, interfaces redesigned, models upgraded. This book is accurate as of May 2026, but specific details — menu locations, exact pricing, feature availability — may have shifted by the time you read this.

The principles, techniques, and strategies in this book have a longer shelf life than the interface details. Writing effective prompts, grounding Copilot in your work context, and integrating it into Microsoft 365 workflows — those skills transfer across versions and across different AI tools.

When something seems different from what's described here, check Microsoft's support site at support.microsoft.com/copilot for the latest information.

Let us get started.

Part I: Getting Started

"The advance of technology is based on making it fit in so that you do not really even notice it, so it is part of everyday life."

— Bill Gates

Chapter 1: What Is Microsoft Copilot?

You have probably heard the buzz. Artificial intelligence is everywhere now — in the news, in conversations at work, in the apps on your phone. But if you have not sat down and used an AI assistant, you might wonder what the fuss is about. That is where Microsoft Copilot comes in, and that is why you are reading this book.

Microsoft Copilot is an AI-powered assistant built by Microsoft. You talk to it in plain English (or dozens of other languages), ask it questions, have it write things, think through problems, generate images, summarize documents, and more. It lives inside the apps you probably already use — Windows, Microsoft Edge, Word, Excel, PowerPoint, Outlook, and Teams — and it is also available as a standalone website and mobile app.

If you have never used an AI tool before, do not worry. This book assumes zero prior experience. By the end of this chapter, you will understand what Copilot is, where it came from, and why it matters for your daily life and work.

The Simple Explanation

Think of Copilot as a knowledgeable assistant who is always available and never tires. You type or speak a question, and it responds with helpful, human-sounding answers. Need a thank-you email drafted? Ask Copilot. Want to understand a complicated news story? Ask Copilot. Trying to plan a vacation itinerary? Ask Copilot.

Unlike a search engine, which hands you a list of links and leaves you to figure things out, Copilot reads through information and gives you a direct, synthesized answer. It can also create things — write essays, compose emails, generate images, build tables, brainstorm ideas, and write code.

Copilot is powered by large language models, a type of artificial intelligence trained on enormous amounts of text from books, websites, articles, and other sources. These models learned patterns in human language well enough to generate new text that reads as if a person wrote it. Microsoft partners with OpenAI to use their most advanced models — specifically the GPT-5 family — to power Copilot.

A Brief History: How We Got Here

Microsoft has been trying to build a useful AI assistant for years. If you used Windows 10, you might remember Cortana, the voice assistant that could set reminders and answer basic questions. Cortana was a solid first attempt, but it never reached the level of usefulness people wanted.

Everything changed in late 2022 and early 2023 when OpenAI released ChatGPT, which captured the world's imagination with its ability to hold natural conversations. Microsoft, which had invested billions in OpenAI, moved quickly. In February 2023, they launched an AI-powered version of their Bing search engine, initially called "Bing Chat."

Bing Chat was impressive. It could answer questions using real-time information from the web, hold extended conversations, and generate images. But the name was limiting — it tied the experience to Bing, which many people did not use as their primary search engine.

So in late 2023, Microsoft made a smart move: they rebranded the experience as "Microsoft Copilot." The new name signaled something important. This was not just a search tool. It was an AI companion — a copilot — designed to work alongside you in everything you do on your computer.

From there, things moved fast. Microsoft embedded Copilot into Windows 11, into the Edge browser, and most importantly, deep into Microsoft 365 — Word, Excel, PowerPoint, Outlook, and Teams. By 2025 and into 2026, Copilot gained what Microsoft calls "agentic capabilities," meaning it can take actions on your behalf, not just answer questions. It can draft documents, manage your calendar, summarize meeting recordings, and automate multi-step workflows.

Where You Can Use Copilot

One of Copilot's strengths is that it meets you where you already are. Here are the main places you will find it:

Copilot on the Web. Visit copilot.microsoft.com in any browser. This is the simplest way to start. You get a chat interface where you can type questions, have conversations, generate images, and more. No installation required.

The Windows App. If you are running Windows 10 or 11, there is a dedicated Copilot app. Pin it to your taskbar for quick access. It works like the web version but feels more integrated with your desktop.

Microsoft Edge. The Edge browser has Copilot built into a sidebar. Ask it questions about the page you are viewing, get summaries of articles, or have a general conversation — all without leaving the page.

Mobile Apps. Copilot is available as a free app on iOS (iPhone and iPad) and Android. The mobile app supports voice conversations, making it easy to talk to Copilot hands-free.

Inside Microsoft 365. This is where Copilot shines for professionals. If you have a Microsoft 365 subscription with Copilot, it appears inside Word, Excel, PowerPoint, Outlook, and Teams. In Word, it drafts and rewrites documents. In Excel, it analyzes data and creates charts. In PowerPoint, it builds entire presentations. In Outlook, it summarizes long email threads and drafts replies. In Teams, it summarizes meetings you missed.

What Can Copilot Actually Do?

Let us get concrete. Here is a sampling of what you can do with Copilot today:

Answer questions. Ask anything from "What is the capital of Mongolia?" to "Explain quantum computing like I am ten years old" to "What are the pros and cons of buying versus leasing a car?"

Search the web with citations. Copilot can search Bing for current information and link to its sources. This is called "search grounding," and it lets you verify what Copilot tells you.

Write and edit text. Need a cover letter? A birthday toast? A business proposal? A complaint letter to your landlord? Tell Copilot what you need, and it drafts it. You can then ask it to revise the tone, shorten it, make it more formal, or adjust it however you like.

Generate images. Copilot creates pictures from text descriptions, powered by OpenAI's GPT Image 1.5 (which began rolling out in January 2026 as the successor to DALL-E 3). Microsoft Designer is a related creative surface for laying those images into templates. Describe what you want — "a cozy cabin in the woods during autumn" — and it generates the image.

Summarize and analyze. Paste in a long article, a contract, or meeting notes, and ask Copilot to summarize the key points. It can pull out action items, identify themes, or highlight potential issues.

Brainstorm and plan. Use Copilot as a thinking partner. Brainstorm names for a business, plan a weekly meal schedule, outline a presentation, or think through a difficult decision.

Have extended conversations. Copilot remembers context within a conversation. You can build on previous messages, refine your requests, and have a back-and-forth dialogue much like you would with a knowledgeable colleague.

Work inside your documents. With the right subscription, Copilot works directly inside your Word documents, Excel spreadsheets, PowerPoint presentations, Outlook emails, and Teams chats. This is where the "copilot" metaphor comes alive — it works alongside you in the tools you already use.

What Copilot Is Not

Setting expectations matters, especially if this is your first experience with AI. Here is what Copilot is not:

It is not infallible. Copilot can and does make mistakes. It may present incorrect information confidently, misunderstand your question, or generate text that sounds right but is factually wrong. Always verify important information, especially anything involving health, legal, or financial matters.

It is not a person. Copilot does not have feelings, opinions, or consciousness. When it says "I think" or "I believe," those are language patterns, not thoughts. It is a tool — an extraordinarily capable one, but a tool.

It is not a replacement for expertise. Copilot can help you draft a legal document, but it is not a lawyer. It can explain medical symptoms, but it is not a doctor. Think of it as a brilliant research assistant, not a licensed professional.

It does not learn from your conversations permanently. Copilot remembers context within a single conversation, but it does not carry memories from one conversation to the next (unless you use specific features designed for that, which we cover later).

It is not free of limitations. Copilot will decline to do certain things — generate harmful content, provide instructions for dangerous activities, or create certain types of images. These guardrails are intentional.

How Is Copilot Different from Other AI Assistants?

You might wonder how Copilot compares to other AI tools you have heard about — ChatGPT, Google Gemini, Claude. Fair question.

The honest answer: the underlying AI capabilities are similar across these tools. They are all powered by large language models, and they all handle basic conversation, writing, and question-answering competently.

Where Copilot stands apart is integration. No other AI assistant is as deeply embedded in the Microsoft ecosystem. If your work life revolves around Word, Excel, PowerPoint, Outlook, and Teams — and for hundreds of millions of people worldwide, it does — then Copilot has a unique advantage. It works with your actual documents, your actual emails, your actual meeting recordings. It understands the context of your work because it lives inside the tools where your work happens.

Copilot also benefits from Bing search integration, which lets it pull current information from the web and provide citations. And its image generation through Microsoft Designer is included at no extra cost for many users.

For people who live in the Microsoft ecosystem, Copilot is the most natural and powerful AI assistant available.

The Technology Behind the Curtain

You do not need the technical details to use Copilot well, but a little context helps.

Copilot is powered by OpenAI's GPT-5 family of models. "GPT" stands for Generative Pre-trained Transformer, the type of AI architecture used. The "5" indicates the fifth major generation. Microsoft uses several variants, including GPT-5.2 (the everyday default) and GPT-5.4 Thinking (available for deeper reasoning since March 2026), each optimized for different tasks.

These models were trained on vast amounts of text, learning patterns in language, facts about the world, and reasoning strategies. When you ask Copilot a question, it does not look up the answer in a database. It generates a response word by word, predicting the most helpful and relevant next word based on what it learned during training.

This is why Copilot is flexible — it is not following a script. It generates fresh responses tailored to your specific request. It is also why it can occasionally produce errors: it is making predictions, not retrieving verified facts.

When Copilot uses Bing search grounding, it supplements its built-in knowledge with real-time information from the web. This combination of deep training and live search makes it useful for both general knowledge and current events.

Why This Matters for You

The bottom line: Microsoft Copilot is one of the most accessible and practical AI tools available today. It is free to start using, it runs on devices you already own, and it integrates with software you probably already use.

Whether you want to save time on writing, get help understanding complex topics, boost your productivity at work, or explore what AI can do, Copilot is an excellent place to start.

In the next chapter, we walk through the different Copilot plans so you can figure out which one fits your needs and budget. Then we get you set up. By the end of this book, you will be using Copilot with confidence — and wondering how you ever got by without it.

Chapter 2: Choosing the Right Plan

One of the first questions people ask about Microsoft Copilot is, "Do I have to pay for it?" The short answer is no — you can start using Copilot right now without spending a dime. The longer answer is that Microsoft offers several plans, and the right one depends on how you plan to use it.

This chapter breaks down every Copilot plan available in 2026, explains what each one includes, and helps you decide which tier fits your situation. No marketing jargon, just honest guidance.

The Free Tier: More Than You Might Expect

The free version of Copilot is useful. This is not a crippled trial designed to frustrate you into upgrading. It is a fully functional AI assistant that millions of people use every day without paying a cent.

Here is what you get with free Copilot:

- **Chat conversations** with GPT-5 class models
- **Bing search grounding** so Copilot can find current information and cite sources
- **Image generation** through Microsoft Designer (with daily limits)
- **Access on all platforms** — web, Windows app, Edge sidebar, iOS, and Android
- **Voice conversations** on mobile
- **Basic file and image analysis** — you can upload a photo or document and ask questions about it

The Free tier has limitations. You get a limited number of messages per day with the more powerful models, and you may be shifted to a lighter model during peak usage. You do not get Copilot inside Microsoft 365 apps, and advanced features like Think Deeper mode carry daily usage caps.

But here is the point: if you are new to AI and want to explore, the Free tier is more than enough. You can use it for weeks or months before you need to think about upgrading.

Best for: Casual users, anyone exploring AI for the first time, students, anyone who wants a capable AI assistant without commitment.

Microsoft 365 Personal: The Solo Bundle

At $9.99 per month (or $99.99 per year), Microsoft 365 Personal is the entry-level paid consumer plan. It covers one person and bundles the full Microsoft 365 suite — Word, Excel, PowerPoint, Outlook, OneNote — with 1 TB of OneDrive storage and Copilot built into those apps.

What you get beyond free Copilot:

- **Copilot inside Microsoft 365 apps** — the AI assistant appears in Word, Excel, PowerPoint, and Outlook, working directly with your documents and email
- **Higher usage** than the Free tier for select Copilot features
- **Full desktop and web Office apps** for a single user
- **1 TB of OneDrive storage** for your files

This is the simplest paid path for an individual who wants Copilot inside their productivity apps without paying for the highest tier.

Best for: Individuals who want Microsoft 365 plus in-app Copilot at the lowest paid price point.

Microsoft 365 Family: The Household Bundle

At $12.99 per month (or $129.99 per year), Microsoft 365 Family extends the Personal bundle across a household of up to six people. Each person gets their own Microsoft 365 apps and 1 TB of OneDrive storage, for 6 TB across the family.

One important detail on Copilot: AI features in the Microsoft 365 apps are available to the **subscription owner only**, not to the additional people sharing the family plan. Everyone gets the apps and storage; only the owner gets Copilot inside Word, Excel, PowerPoint, and Outlook.

What you get beyond free Copilot:

- **Copilot inside Microsoft 365 apps** for the subscription owner
- **Higher usage** than the Free tier for select Copilot features

- **Microsoft 365 apps for up to six people**
- **6 TB of OneDrive storage total** (1 TB per person)

Best for: Households that want to share Microsoft 365 across multiple people while giving the subscription owner in-app Copilot.

Microsoft 365 Premium: The Top Consumer Tier

At $19.99 per month (or $199.99 per year), Microsoft 365 Premium is the top consumer tier, sitting above Personal and Family. Like Family, it covers up to six people, with AI features reserved for the subscription owner. What Premium adds is the most generous Copilot usage of the three consumer plans — plus a capability the lower tiers do not include: AI agents that can take on more complex tasks, like producing source-cited research reports.

Across the three consumer plans, AI usage limits scale up: Personal and Family offer “higher usage” than the Free tier for select Copilot features, while Premium offers “extensive usage” — the highest consumer allowance.

What Premium adds beyond Personal and Family:

- **Extensive usage** for select Copilot features — the most generous limits of any consumer plan
- **AI agents for complex tasks** — e.g., source-cited research reports that go beyond simple chat
- **Priority access** to the latest and most powerful models
- **Microsoft 365 apps for up to six people** (AI for the subscription owner)
- **6 TB of OneDrive storage total** (1 TB per person)

If you are a heavy Copilot user, or you want the agent capabilities, Premium is the consumer plan to pick.

Best for: Heavy Copilot users, households that want the highest consumer AI limits, and anyone who wants AI agents for complex research and multi-step tasks.

Microsoft 365 Copilot for Business: The Workplace Solution

Now we move into business territory. Microsoft 365 Copilot for Business runs $18 to $21 per user per month (on top of an existing Microsoft 365 business subscription) and is designed for small to mid-sized businesses.

This tier includes everything from the consumer plans plus:

- **Copilot deeply integrated into business Microsoft 365** – Word, Excel, PowerPoint, Outlook, Teams, and more
- **Access to organizational data** – Copilot can search across your company's SharePoint sites, emails, Teams messages, and documents to find relevant information
- **Meeting intelligence** – Copilot can attend Teams meetings, take notes, identify action items, and generate meeting summaries
- **Business-grade security and compliance** – your data stays within your organization's Microsoft 365 tenant and is not used to train AI models
- **Admin controls** – IT administrators can manage who has access and set usage policies
- **Copilot Studio access** – basic ability to customize and extend Copilot with company-specific knowledge

The business tier is purchased and managed by your organization, not by you individually. If your company runs on Microsoft 365 and is considering Copilot, this is likely the tier they would choose.

Best for: Small and mid-sized businesses that run on Microsoft 365 and want to boost team productivity.

Microsoft 365 Copilot Enterprise: The Full Package

At $30 per user per month (on top of an existing Microsoft 365 enterprise subscription), the Enterprise tier is the most comprehensive Copilot offering. It includes everything in the Business tier plus:

- **Enterprise-grade data protection** with the most stringent security and compliance controls

- **Microsoft 365 Graph grounding** — Copilot can reason across your entire organization's data, understanding relationships between people, documents, emails, meetings, and more
- **Advanced Copilot Studio** — full access to build custom copilots, plugins, and agents tailored to your organization's specific workflows
- **Agentic capabilities** — Copilot can take multi-step actions on behalf of users, automating complex workflows
- **Usage analytics and reporting** for administrators
- **Priority support** from Microsoft

This tier is built for large organizations with complex needs and strict compliance requirements. If you work at a company with hundreds or thousands of employees, this is likely the version your IT department would deploy.

Best for: Large enterprises with complex data environments, strict compliance needs, and the desire to build custom AI solutions.

A Quick Word About GitHub Copilot

You may have heard about "GitHub Copilot" and wondered if it is the same thing. It is not. GitHub Copilot is a separate product built for software developers. It helps programmers write code by suggesting completions, generating functions, and explaining existing code.

GitHub Copilot has its own pricing with five tiers: Free, Pro ($10/month), Pro+ ($39/month for individuals), Business ($19/user/month), and Enterprise ($39/user/month). Pro+ and Enterprise share the $39 price point but serve different audiences — Pro+ is for individual developers who want premium features, while Enterprise is a per-user organizational plan with compliance controls, fine-tuned models, and admin management. Chapter 24 covers GitHub Copilot in detail.

Unless you are a software developer, you do not need to worry about GitHub Copilot. This book focuses on the general-purpose Microsoft Copilot anyone can use.

How to Decide: A Practical Framework

Still not sure which plan is right for you? Walk through these questions:

Question 1: Are you just curious about AI? Start with the Free tier. There is zero risk, and you will get a solid feel for what Copilot can do. You can always upgrade later.

Question 2: Do you use Microsoft 365 (Word, Excel, PowerPoint, Outlook)? If yes, and you want Copilot to work inside those apps, you need a paid Microsoft 365 plan — Personal ($9.99/month), Family ($12.99/month), or Premium ($19.99/month). All three include Copilot in the apps; the differences are the number of people covered and how generous the AI usage limits are.

Question 3: Which consumer plan — Personal, Family, or Premium? Pick based on how heavily you use Copilot and how many people will share the subscription. Personal is the cheapest path to in-app Copilot for one person. Family covers up to six people with the same Copilot allowance, but only the subscription owner gets the AI features. Premium is the top tier: highest usage limits and AI agents for complex tasks like source-cited research reports. If you hit the Free tier's limits regularly — running out of daily messages, getting bumped to a lighter model, or wanting more Think Deeper conversations — Premium is the consumer plan to pick.

Question 4: Is this for your business? Talk to your IT department or Microsoft sales representative about the Business ($18–21/user/month) or Enterprise ($30/user/month) tiers. These are organizational decisions, not individual ones.

Question 5: Do you want to try before you commit? Microsoft frequently offers free trials of the Microsoft 365 consumer plans — Personal, Family, and Premium. Check the current offers at copilot.microsoft.com before committing to a paid plan.

A Note on Plan Names and Pricing

Plan names, pricing, and feature bundles described in this chapter reflect May 2026. Microsoft reorganizes its consumer and business offerings regularly — renaming plans, adjusting price points, or shifting features between tiers. Before making a purchasing decision, check the current plans at copilot.microsoft.com and microsoft.com/microsoft-365.

The Bottom Line on Pricing

A candid assessment. The Free tier is surprisingly good, and most casual users will be happy with it. If you want Copilot inside Word, Excel, PowerPoint, and Outlook, the cheapest path is Microsoft 365 Personal at $9.99 per month – one person, full Office suite, in-app Copilot. Microsoft 365 Family at $12.99 per month adds the same apps for up to six people (with AI features for the subscription owner). Microsoft 365 Premium at $19.99 per month is the top consumer tier: the most generous Copilot usage and AI agents that can handle complex tasks like source-cited research reports.

The business and enterprise tiers are a different category entirely. They are not impulse purchases – they are organizational investments. For companies that run on Microsoft 365, the productivity gains can be substantial.

One last piece of advice: start free, use Copilot for a few weeks, then decide if you want more. There is no penalty for starting at the bottom and working your way up. The next chapter walks you through setting up your account, regardless of which plan you choose.

Chapter 3: Setting Up Your Account

You have decided to give Microsoft Copilot a try — great. Now let us get you set up. This chapter walks you through creating or connecting your account, installing the apps you need, and configuring Copilot so it is ready to use on every device you own.

Setup is straightforward. If you already have a Microsoft account — and you probably do, even if you do not realize it — you are halfway there.

Do You Already Have a Microsoft Account?

Before you create anything new, check whether you already have a Microsoft account. If you have ever used any of the following, you have one:

- A Hotmail, Outlook.com, or Live.com email address
- Xbox Live or an Xbox console
- Windows with a sign-in (not a local-only account)
- Microsoft 365, OneDrive, or Skype
- A Microsoft Store purchase

If any of those ring a bell, you have a Microsoft account. Sign in to Copilot with those same credentials — no new account needed.

If you use a work or school computer, you likely also have a Microsoft organizational account (sometimes called a "work or school account"). This is separate from your personal Microsoft account, and it matters because Copilot's behavior and available features differ depending on which account you use. More on this shortly.

Creating a New Microsoft Account

If you do not have a Microsoft account, creating one takes about two minutes:

1. Open any web browser and go to **account.microsoft.com**.
2. Click **Create a Microsoft account** (or **Sign up**).

3. You can use an existing email address (like your Gmail or Yahoo address) or create a new Outlook.com email address for free.
4. Choose a password. Make it strong — at least 12 characters with a mix of letters, numbers, and symbols.
5. Microsoft will send a verification code to your email or phone. Enter the code to confirm your account.
6. Fill in basic profile information (name, country, date of birth).
7. You are done.

That is it. You now have a Microsoft account that works with Copilot, OneDrive, Outlook.com, and every other Microsoft service.

A note about security: Set up two-factor authentication on your Microsoft account right away. Go to account.microsoft.com, navigate to Security settings, and enable it. This adds a second verification step at sign-in — typically a code sent to your phone — and dramatically reduces the risk of someone else accessing your account.

Accessing Copilot on the Web

The fastest way to start using Copilot is through your web browser:

1. Go to **copilot.microsoft.com**.
2. You will see the Copilot chat interface. You can start chatting immediately without signing in, but your conversations will not be saved.
3. Click **Sign in** in the upper right corner and enter your Microsoft account credentials.
4. Once signed in, your conversations save to your account, and you get access to every feature included in your plan.

That is all it takes. Bookmark this page and come back anytime.

On the Free tier, you are ready to go. To upgrade to a paid plan, look for the upgrade option in the interface — it guides you through selecting a plan and entering payment information.

Setting Up Copilot on Windows

If you are running Windows 11, Copilot is either already installed or can be installed quickly:

On Windows 11 (version 23H2 and later):

1. Look for the Copilot icon in your taskbar — it looks like a stylized ribbon or wave shape. If you see it, click it and sign in with your Microsoft account.
2. If you do not see the icon, open the Microsoft Store (search for "Microsoft Store" in the Start menu), search for "Microsoft Copilot," and install the app.
3. Once installed, you can pin it to your taskbar for quick access. Right-click the Copilot icon in the Start menu and select **Pin to taskbar**.
4. Sign in with your Microsoft account, and you are set.

On Windows 10:

Copilot is available as a downloadable app from the Microsoft Store. Search for "Microsoft Copilot," install it, and sign in. The experience mirrors the web version, running in its own window.

Keyboard shortcut: On many Windows 11 systems, **Windows key + C** opens Copilot (though this shortcut may vary depending on system configuration and Windows version). Check your keyboard settings if it does not work.

Setting Up Copilot in Microsoft Edge

If you use Microsoft Edge as your web browser, Copilot is built right into the sidebar:

1. Open Microsoft Edge.
2. Look for the Copilot icon in the upper right corner of the browser, near the address bar. It uses the same wave-shaped icon.
3. Click it to open the Copilot sidebar.
4. Sign in with your Microsoft account if prompted.

The Edge sidebar is useful because it interacts with the page you are viewing. Ask it to summarize an article, explain something on the page, or answer questions about what you are reading — all without leaving the page.

If you do not see the Copilot icon in Edge, make sure your browser is up to date. Go to **Settings** > **About Microsoft Edge** and install any available updates.

Setting Up Copilot on Your Phone

Copilot is available as a free app for both iPhone and Android:

On iPhone or iPad: 1. Open the App Store. 2. Search for "Microsoft Copilot." 3. Download and install the app. 4. Open it and sign in with your Microsoft account.

On Android: 1. Open the Google Play Store. 2. Search for "Microsoft Copilot." 3. Download and install the app. 4. Open it and sign in with your Microsoft account.

The mobile app supports text chat, voice conversations (tap the microphone icon), and image input (use your camera to show Copilot something and ask about it). Same Copilot, optimized for your phone's screen.

Setting Up Copilot in Microsoft 365

If you have a Microsoft 365 subscription with Copilot capabilities (a paid consumer plan — Microsoft 365 Personal, Family, or Premium — or a business/enterprise plan), Copilot will appear inside your Office apps:

In Word, Excel, PowerPoint, and Outlook (desktop apps):

1. Make sure your Microsoft 365 apps are up to date. Open any Office app, go to **File** > **Account** > **Update Options** > **Update Now**.
2. Sign in with the Microsoft account that has Copilot access. Go to **File** > **Account** and verify you are signed in with the correct account.
3. Look for the Copilot icon in the ribbon (the toolbar at the top of the application). In Word, it typically appears in the Home tab. In Excel, it appears in the Home tab as well.
4. Click the Copilot icon to open the Copilot pane.

If you do not see the Copilot icon, a few things might be going on:

- Your apps may need updating. Microsoft 365 apps update automatically, but updates are sometimes delayed.
- You may be signed in with the wrong account. If you have both a personal and work account, make sure the account with Copilot access is active.
- Your subscription may not include Copilot. Check your subscription status at account.microsoft.com.
- If this is a work account, your IT administrator may not have enabled Copilot for your organization yet.

In the web versions of Office (Word Online, Excel Online, etc.):

1. Go to **microsoft365.com** and sign in.
2. Open any document in Word Online, Excel Online, or PowerPoint Online.
3. Look for the Copilot icon in the toolbar. It works the same way as in the desktop apps.

In Microsoft Teams:

1. Open Teams (desktop app or web version).
2. Look for the Copilot icon in the left sidebar or in the chat area.
3. During meetings, Copilot can be activated to transcribe and summarize the discussion. Look for the Copilot option in the meeting controls.

Configuring Your Preferences

Once signed in, take a few minutes to configure Copilot to work the way you want:

Conversation history. By default, Copilot saves your conversations so you can return to them later. Manage your history by clicking your profile icon and looking for conversation history or privacy settings. Disable saving if you prefer.

Search personalization. Copilot uses Bing for web searches and can personalize results based on your location and search history. Adjust this in settings — decide whether you want personalized results or prefer more generic responses.

Tone and style. You cannot set a permanent tone preference, but later chapters show you how to guide Copilot's communication style through your prompts.

Notifications. If you are using Copilot in Microsoft 365, you can configure whether Copilot proactively suggests things (like email replies in Outlook) or waits for you to ask.

Personal Account vs. Work Account: What Is the Difference?

This trips people up, so let us clear it up.

Personal Microsoft account (the one you use for Outlook.com, Xbox, or personal Microsoft 365): with this account, you get the consumer version of Copilot. Your conversations are private to you. Available features depend on your personal subscription level (free, Personal, Family, or Premium).

Work or school account (the one your employer or school issued, typically ending in your organization's domain): with this account, you get the business or enterprise version. Copilot can access your organization's data — emails, files in SharePoint, Teams conversations — which makes it more powerful in a work context. Your IT administrator controls what Copilot can access and which features are available.

Most Copilot interfaces let you switch between accounts. Click your profile icon or avatar to see account-switching options. Some people use Copilot with both accounts — personal for personal tasks, work for professional tasks.

Troubleshooting Common Setup Issues

Solutions to the most common setup problems:

"I cannot sign in." Check your email address and password. If you have forgotten your password, click "Forgot password" and follow the recovery steps. If two-factor authentication is enabled, make sure you have access to your authentication method (phone, authenticator app, etc.).

"Copilot is not available in my country." As of 2026, Copilot is available in most countries, but some features are limited in certain regions. Check Microsoft's official documentation for current availability.

"I signed in but I do not see premium features." Make sure your subscription is active. Go to account.microsoft.com and check your subscriptions page. If you just subscribed, sign out and back in — it sometimes takes a few minutes for the subscription to activate.

"Copilot in Word/Excel is not showing up." Update your Microsoft 365 apps, verify you are signed in with the correct account, and make sure your subscription includes Copilot. If this is a work account, contact your IT administrator.

"The mobile app is not working." Make sure your phone's operating system is up to date and you have a stable internet connection. Copilot requires an internet connection — it does not function offline.

A Quick Security Checklist

Before you start using Copilot regularly, take care of these security basics:

1. **Enable two-factor authentication** on your Microsoft account.
2. **Use a strong, unique password** — not one you reuse elsewhere.
3. **Be cautious about what you share.** Do not paste passwords, social security numbers, credit card numbers, or other highly sensitive information into Copilot conversations.
4. **Review your privacy settings.** Visit your Microsoft privacy dashboard at account.microsoft.com/privacy to see what data Microsoft collects and adjust your preferences.
5. **Log out on shared computers.** If you use Copilot on a public or shared computer, always sign out when you are done.

You Are Ready to Go

At this point, you should have Copilot set up on at least one device and be signed in with your Microsoft account. If you have a paid subscription, you should also have access to the premium features in your plan.

In the next chapter, we look under the hood at the AI models and conversation modes that power Copilot. Understanding these helps you get better results from every interaction — you will know when to use the quick, snappy mode versus when to engage Copilot's deep reasoning.

Chapter 4: Understanding Copilot's Models and Modes

Now that you have Copilot set up, you might be tempted to jump right in. And you can — Copilot works well out of the box. But taking a few minutes to understand what is happening behind the scenes will make you a more effective user. Knowing which model is handling your request and which conversation mode to choose is the difference between a decent answer and a great one.

This chapter explains the AI models that power Copilot, the three conversation modes, and when to use each one. Think of it as learning how to shift gears before you start driving.

What Are AI Models, and Why Do They Matter?

When you send a message to Copilot, your words are processed by an AI model — software trained on enormous amounts of text to understand and generate human language. The model reads your input, figures out what you are asking, and generates a response.

Not all models are equal. Some are smaller and faster, optimized for quick responses. Others are larger and more powerful, capable of more nuanced reasoning but slower to respond. Microsoft uses several models from OpenAI's GPT-5 family, and understanding the differences helps you get the best results.

GPT-5.2: The Everyday Workhorse

GPT-5.2 is the baseline model in the GPT-5 family. It is highly capable — far more advanced than the models behind the first versions of Copilot in 2023 — and it handles the vast majority of tasks with ease. When you ask Copilot a straightforward question, draft a quick email, or brainstorm ideas, GPT-5.2 is likely doing the work.

This model is fast. Responses come back in seconds, and for most everyday tasks, the quality is excellent. Think of GPT-5.2 as the reliable daily driver that gets you where you need to go.

GPT-5.4: The Premium Engine

GPT-5.4 is the more powerful sibling. It brings gains in reasoning, accuracy, nuance, and the ability to handle complex instructions. When a task requires sophistication — a detailed analysis, a multi-part question, complex data, or polished creative writing — GPT-5.4 excels.

On a paid plan, Copilot uses GPT-5.4 more often, and you get priority access during busy periods. Free users may be served GPT-5.2 when demand is high so everyone can keep accessing the service.

GPT-5.4 Thinking: The Deep Reasoner

GPT-5.4 Thinking is a specialized variant built for extended reasoning. Instead of generating a quick response, it "thinks" through problems step by step before answering. It takes longer — sometimes 30 seconds or more — but the reasoning is substantially better on complex tasks.

This is the model behind Copilot's "Think Deeper" mode, covered shortly. It is particularly valuable for:

- Math and logic problems
- Multi-step planning
- Complex analysis and comparison
- Technical problem-solving
- Any question where a thoughtful, carefully reasoned answer is more important than a fast one

Think of GPT-5.4 Thinking as the specialist you bring in when the stakes are high and you want someone to think it through carefully. Microsoft is also rolling out GPT-5.5 Thinking — a newer reasoning model with stronger instruction following — to selected Copilot surfaces (Copilot Chat, Word, Excel, PowerPoint), so on those surfaces Think Deeper may already be running on the newer model.

The Three Conversation Modes

Copilot offers three conversation modes you can select before or during a conversation. Each tells Copilot how to approach your request. Here is what they are and when to use each.

Auto Mode: Let Copilot Decide

Auto is the default mode, and for most people most of the time, it is the right choice. Copilot analyzes your message and decides how to handle it. Simple questions get quick responses. Complex questions get more thoughtful treatment. Copilot decides whether to search the web, which model to use, and how much reasoning to apply.

When to use Auto mode: - Most of the time - When you are not sure which mode would be best - When your requests vary in complexity throughout a conversation - When you want Copilot to "just figure it out"

Auto mode adapts well. Ask "What time is it in Tokyo?" and you get a quick answer. Follow up with "Help me plan a two-week itinerary for Japan with a mix of cultural sites and nature experiences," and it shifts to a more thoughtful approach. You do not have to manage the gears — Copilot does it for you.

Quick Response Mode: Speed Over Depth

Quick Response mode prioritizes speed. It tells Copilot to deliver an answer as fast as possible, without extra time on reasoning or searching. Responses are shorter, more direct, and arrive almost instantly.

When to use Quick Response mode: - Simple factual questions: "What year was the Eiffel Tower built?" - Quick translations: "How do you say 'thank you' in Japanese?" - Basic calculations: "What is 15% of 340?" - Simple definitions: "What is photosynthesis?" - When you want a fast answer and do not need depth or nuance - When you are in a hurry and a "good enough" answer is fine

When not to use Quick Response mode: - Complex questions that require analysis - Tasks where accuracy is critical - Creative writing where quality matters - Multi-step problems

Think of Quick Response as the express lane at the grocery store. Faster, but built for small, simple transactions.

Think Deeper Mode: Maximum Reasoning Power

Think Deeper mode is the opposite of Quick Response. It engages GPT-5.4 Thinking, the extended reasoning model, and tells Copilot to take its time and work through your request carefully. You will see a "thinking" indicator while Copilot processes, and responses can take 30 seconds to a minute or more.

The results are noticeably better on the right kinds of tasks.

When to use Think Deeper mode: - Complex analytical questions: "Compare the economic policies of these three countries and analyze which approach would work best for a small island nation." - Math and logic problems: "Walk me through this statistics problem step by step." - Strategic planning: "I am starting a small bakery. Help me think through the financial considerations for my first year." - Debugging arguments: "Here is my business proposal. What are the weaknesses in my reasoning?" - Legal or technical document analysis: "Review this contract clause and explain what it means in plain language." - Any time you want Copilot to think carefully rather than respond quickly

When Think Deeper is overkill: - Simple questions with straightforward answers - Quick tasks like drafting a short email - Casual conversation or brainstorming where speed matters more than depth

Think Deeper is like asking someone to sit down, take out a notepad, and work through a problem instead of giving you an off-the-cuff answer. The answer takes longer, but it is more thorough and more reliable.

A note on availability: Think Deeper uses significantly more computational resources than the other modes. The free plan caps Think Deeper queries per day. Paid plans offer more generous allowances, with Microsoft 365 Premium users getting the highest consumer limits.

How to Switch Between Modes

Switching modes is simple:

On the web (copilot.microsoft.com): Look for the mode selector near the text input area, usually displayed as a dropdown or a set of buttons. Click to switch between Auto, Quick Response, and Think Deeper.

On the Windows app: Same approach — look for the mode selector near where you type your messages.

On mobile: The mode selector is typically accessible via an icon near the text input field. Tap it to see your options.

Mid-conversation: You can switch modes at any point. If you start in Auto and realize you need deeper reasoning, switch to Think Deeper for your next message. The conversation context is preserved.

Choosing the Right Mode: A Decision Framework

A simple framework for choosing the right mode:

1. **Start with Auto.** It handles most situations well and adapts automatically.
2. **Switch to Quick Response** when you need fast, simple answers and do not want to wait.
3. **Switch to Think Deeper** when accuracy, thoroughness, or careful reasoning matters more than speed.

Over time, you will develop an intuition for which mode fits which situation. Do not overthink it — the difference is real but not dramatic for most everyday tasks. The biggest gains from Think Deeper come on genuinely complex problems.

How Web Search Grounding Works

Regardless of which mode you use, Copilot can search the web using Bing. This is called "search grounding," and it is one of Copilot's most important features.

When you ask a question that benefits from current information — news, prices, weather, recent events, factual data — Copilot automatically searches the web, reads through relevant results, and incorporates that information into its response. It also provides citations — numbered references that link to the sources — so you can verify the information yourself.

This matters. Without web search, AI models can only draw on what they learned during training, which means they can be out of date or lack specific factual information. With search grounding, Copilot delivers current, verifiable information.

You do not need to tell Copilot to search the web. In Auto mode, it decides automatically whether a search would help. But you can explicitly ask: "Search the web for the latest reviews of the Samsung Galaxy S26" or "What does the New York Times say about the new climate bill?"

When Copilot uses web search, you will see numbered citations in its response, like [1], [2], [3]. Click or tap these to see the source URLs. Always check sources when accuracy matters.

Pages: The Collaborative AI Canvas

If you have a paid plan, you have access to Pages — a feature that takes AI conversations beyond the chat format. A Page is a document you and Copilot create together. Instead of a back-and-forth chat, you get an editable canvas where Copilot's output appears as formatted text you can edit, rearrange, and build upon.

Pages are particularly useful for:

- Longer writing projects where you want to iterate on a document
- Research summaries you want to organize and refine
- Planning documents where you want to keep adding sections
- Collaborative work you want to share with others

Think of Pages as a bridge between a chat and a real document. You get the AI assistance of chat with the editability and structure of a word processor.

Notebooks: Extended Context

Notebooks, also on paid plans, let you work with longer inputs. Standard chat has limits on how much text you can include in a single message. Notebooks extend that limit significantly, letting you paste in longer documents, articles, or data sets and ask Copilot to work with them.

If you need to analyze a lengthy report, summarize a long article, or work with a large amount of text, Notebooks are the right tool.

Putting It All Together

A practical example of how understanding models and modes makes you more effective:

Imagine you are researching a major purchase — say, a new car. You start in Auto mode and ask, “What are the most reliable midsize SUVs in 2026?” Copilot searches the web and gives you a solid overview with citations.

You want more detail. Switch to Think Deeper and ask, “Compare the Toyota RAV4, Honda CR-V, and Mazda CX-50. Consider reliability, resale value, fuel efficiency, technology features, and total cost of ownership over five years. Which one is the best value?”

Copilot takes a minute to think it through and returns a detailed, well-reasoned comparison, citing several automotive review sites and consumer reports.

Later, you want a quick fact: “What is the cargo space of the RAV4 in cubic feet?” Switch to Quick Response and get your answer in two seconds.

Same conversation, three different modes, each appropriate for the task at hand. That is how understanding models and modes makes you a more effective Copilot user.

What You Will Learn Next

Now that you understand the engine under the hood, it is time to drive. In Chapter 5, we have your first real conversations with Copilot. You will learn how to write effective prompts, refine Copilot’s responses, and develop the back-and-forth dialogue that gets the best results. This is where Copilot goes from interesting to useful.

Chapter 5: Your First Conversations

You are set up, you understand the modes, and you are ready to start talking to Copilot. This is where things get fun. But there is a skill to productive conversations with an AI assistant, and learning it early will save you frustration and produce dramatically better results.

This chapter teaches you how to write effective prompts, refine responses, and develop the back-and-forth dialogue that turns Copilot from a novelty into a useful tool.

Your Very First Message

Let us start simple. Open Copilot on whatever device you prefer — the website, the Windows app, the mobile app, or the Edge sidebar. Sign in, and type something like:

> What can you help me with?

Copilot will respond with an overview of its capabilities. This is a fine way to start, but it is a bit like walking into a restaurant and asking, "What do you serve?" You get a general answer when you would do better by looking at the menu and ordering something specific.

So let us try something more concrete:

> I need to write a thank-you note to my neighbor who watched my dog while I was on vacation. She has two cats and was a little nervous about watching a large dog. Make it warm and genuine.

Now Copilot has something to work with. It knows the purpose (thank-you note), the context (dog-sitting, neighbor has cats, was nervous), and the tone (warm, genuine). It will generate a note you can use as-is or tweak to fit your voice.

That is the pattern: give Copilot enough context to produce something useful on the first try.

The Anatomy of a Good Prompt

A "prompt" is the message you send to Copilot. The quality of your prompt directly affects the quality of the response. Here is what makes a prompt effective:

Be Specific About What You Want

Vague prompts get vague responses. Compare these:

Vague: "Tell me about dogs." **Specific:** "What are the best dog breeds for families with young children who live in apartments? I want a breed that is good with kids, does not need a huge yard, and does not shed excessively."

The second prompt gives Copilot clear criteria. The response will be focused, practical, and immediately useful.

Provide Context

Copilot does not know your situation unless you tell it. The more relevant context you provide, the better the response:

Without context: "Help me write an email." **With context:** "Help me write an email to my team of six people announcing that we are switching from Slack to Microsoft Teams. Some people will be resistant to the change. I want to acknowledge their concerns while explaining the benefits. Keep the tone professional but empathetic."

Specify the Format

If you want your response in a particular format, say so:

- "Give me a bulleted list of..."
- "Explain this in three short paragraphs."
- "Create a table comparing..."
- "Write this as a step-by-step guide with numbered instructions."
- "Summarize this in two sentences."

Specify the Tone

Copilot can adapt its writing style to suit your needs:

- "Write this in a casual, conversational tone."
- "Keep it formal and professional."
- "Make it friendly but not too informal."
- "Write it as if you are explaining to a five-year-old."
- "Use an academic tone with precise language."

Specify the Audience

Who is this for? Telling Copilot the intended audience helps it calibrate complexity, vocabulary, and tone:

- "Explain this for someone with no technical background."
- "Write this for experienced project managers."
- "My audience is high school students."
- "This is for a board of directors presentation."

The Power of Follow-Up Messages

Here is something many people miss: the conversation does not end with Copilot's first response. The first response is often just the starting point.

Copilot remembers everything said in the current conversation. You can build on previous messages, ask for changes, and refine the output through follow-up messages. This is "iterating," and it is one of the most powerful techniques you can learn.

An example of how iteration works:

You: "Write a short bio for me. I am a marketing manager with 12 years of experience, I specialize in digital marketing and brand strategy, and I have an MBA from the University of Michigan."

Copilot: *[Generates a professional bio]*

You: "Good start, but make it warmer and less corporate. Add that I am passionate about mentoring junior marketers and that I volunteer as a marketing consultant for local nonprofits."

Copilot: *[Revises the bio with a warmer tone and the additional details]*

You: "Perfect. Now create a shorter version of this — just two to three sentences — that I can use for a conference speaker introduction."

Copilot: *[Creates a condensed version]*

You: "Great. Now make an even shorter version for my X (formerly Twitter) bio. Under 160 characters."

Copilot: *[Creates an ultra-short version]*

Notice what happened. You started with a general request, then refined it through four messages. Each version built on the last. You did not re-explain your background each time — Copilot remembered the context. This is how experienced users work with Copilot.

Common Follow-Up Phrases That Work Well

Keep these phrases in your back pocket. They are useful for refining Copilot's responses:

- **"Make it shorter." / "Make it longer."**
- **"Make it more formal." / "Make it more casual."**
- **"Can you simplify this?"**
- **"Add more detail about [specific topic]."**
- **"Remove the part about [specific thing]."**
- **"Rewrite this as bullet points." / "Rewrite this as a narrative."**
- **"Give me three alternative versions."**
- **"What did you mean by [specific phrase]?"**
- **"Can you give me an example?"**
- **"That is not quite what I meant. I was looking for [clarification]."**
- **"Keep everything the same but change the tone to be more [adjective]."**

Starting a New Conversation

Each conversation with Copilot is independent. When you start a new conversation (by clicking "New chat" or the equivalent), Copilot starts fresh with no memory of previous conversations.

This matters. If you had a great conversation yesterday about planning a trip to Italy, and you start a new chat today and say, "Tell me more about the hotels," Copilot will have no idea what you mean. You will need to re-establish the context.

When to start a new conversation: - When you are switching to a completely different topic - When the current conversation has gotten long and Copilot seems to be losing track of earlier details - When you want a fresh perspective without the influence of previous messages

When to continue an existing conversation: - When you are still working on the same topic or task - When you want to build on something Copilot already generated - When you need Copilot to remember context from earlier in the discussion

Asking Questions Effectively

Copilot excels at answering questions, but how you ask matters. A few patterns that consistently produce good results:

The "Explain Like I Am a Beginner" Pattern

> "Explain how blockchain works. Assume I have no technical background."

This tells Copilot to avoid jargon and use simple analogies.

The "Compare and Contrast" Pattern

> "Compare renting versus buying a home. Include financial considerations, lifestyle factors, and long-term implications. Present this as a pros and cons list for each option."

This produces structured, balanced analysis.

The "Devil's Advocate" Pattern

> "I am thinking about quitting my job to start a freelance business. Give me the strongest arguments against doing this."

This is great for stress-testing decisions. Copilot will not just tell you what you want to hear.

The "Step-by-Step" Pattern

> "Walk me through how to set up a monthly household budget, step by step. I have never done this before."

This produces clear, sequential instructions.

The "Summarize This" Pattern

You can paste a long article, email thread, or document into the chat and ask:

> "Summarize the key points of this article in five bullet points."

This is one of Copilot's most useful capabilities.

What to Do When Copilot Gets It Wrong

Copilot will sometimes give you incorrect information, misunderstand your question, or produce something that is not quite what you wanted. This is normal. How to handle it:

Correct it directly. If Copilot makes a factual error, tell it:

> "That is not right. The Battle of Gettysburg was in 1863, not 1864. Please correct your response."

Copilot will acknowledge the correction and adjust.

Clarify your intent. If the response is off-base, the problem might be ambiguity in your original prompt:

> "I think you misunderstood my question. I was not asking about the history of the company. I wanted to know about their current product lineup."

Ask it to try again. Sometimes the simplest approach works:

> "That response was not quite what I was looking for. Can you try again with a different approach?"

Check the sources. When Copilot cites web sources (those numbered references like [1], [2]), click through to verify. If the sources do not support what Copilot said, let it know.

Know when to be skeptical. Be especially cautious with: - Specific numbers, statistics, and dates - Legal, medical, or financial advice - Claims about specific people or organizations - Anything that sounds too specific to be generated from general knowledge

Working with Files and Images

Copilot can work with files and images you share with it. You can:

Upload an image and ask about it: > "What kind of plant is this?" (with a photo attached) > "Can you read the text in this screenshot?" > "What is wrong with the layout of this design?"

Paste text from a document: Copy text from any source — a PDF, a website, a Word document — and paste it into the chat with your question.

Upload a file directly: In most Copilot interfaces, you can click an attachment icon to upload a file. Copilot reads and analyzes documents, spreadsheets, and other file types.

Practical Exercises to Build Your Skills

The best way to get comfortable with Copilot is to practice. Five exercises to try right now:

Exercise 1: Simple Question Ask Copilot something you have been curious about. Notice how it provides context and nuance beyond a simple factual answer.

Exercise 2: Write Something Ask Copilot to draft something you actually need — an email, a social media post, a message to a friend. Then use follow-up messages to refine it until it sounds like you.

Exercise 3: Explain a Concept Pick something you have always found confusing — insurance deductibles, how Wi-Fi works, the difference between a Roth and traditional IRA — and ask Copilot to explain it in simple terms.

Exercise 4: Summarize Something Find a long article online, copy the text, paste it into Copilot, and ask for a summary. Compare the summary to the original and notice how well it captures the key points.

Exercise 5: Iterate Ask Copilot to write a short paragraph about your hometown. Then spend five follow-up messages refining it — change the tone, add details, make it shorter, change the audience. This exercise teaches the power of iteration.

A Note on Privacy in Conversations

Everything you type to Copilot is sent to Microsoft's servers for processing. Microsoft has privacy protections in place, but be thoughtful about what you share:

- Do not share passwords, social security numbers, or financial account numbers.
- Be cautious with confidential business information unless you are using an enterprise plan with data protection guarantees.
- Conversations may be stored (check your privacy settings if this concerns you).
- If you are using a work account, your organization's data policies apply.

What You Will Learn Next

You now have the foundational skills for productive conversations with Copilot. In the next chapter, we focus on one of the most common and valuable use cases: writing. Whether you need emails, reports, creative content, or anything else involving words on a page, Chapter 6 shows you how to use Copilot as your personal writing assistant.

Part II: Everyday Use

"It is not enough to do your best; you must know what to do, and then do your best."

— W. Edwards Deming

Chapter 6: Writing with Copilot

If there is one thing Copilot does exceptionally well, it is writing. Whether you need to dash off a quick email, draft a formal report, compose a heartfelt letter, or create content for a website, Copilot helps you write faster, more clearly, and with less stress.

This chapter covers how to use Copilot for every kind of writing task — from everyday communication to polished professional documents. You will learn techniques for getting great first drafts, refining tone and style, overcoming writer's block, and using Copilot inside Word for those with Microsoft 365 integration.

Why Copilot Is a Great Writing Partner

Let us be honest: writing is hard for most people. Not because they lack ideas, but because turning ideas into clear, well-organized text takes time and effort. This is where Copilot excels.

Copilot can generate a solid first draft in seconds. That draft will not be perfect — you will almost always want to revise and personalize it — but it gives you something to work with instead of a blank page. That is enormous. The hardest part of writing is often getting started. Copilot removes that barrier.

Beyond first drafts, Copilot can edit your existing writing, suggest improvements, shift tone, restructure arguments, fix grammar, and help you say what you mean more clearly. Think of it as a patient, always-available writing coach.

Everyday Email

Email is probably the most common writing task for most people, and it is where Copilot saves you the most time on a daily basis.

Drafting Emails from Scratch

Tell Copilot who you are writing to, what you need to communicate, and what tone you want:

> "Write a professional email to my colleague Sarah asking if she can cover my shift on Friday. I have a doctor's appointment I cannot reschedule. Keep it friendly and brief."

Copilot produces a ready-to-send email. Review it, tweak anything that does not sound like you, and send.

For more complex emails:

> "Write an email to my client, David Chen at Meridian Corp, following up on our meeting last Tuesday. We discussed three options for their website redesign. Remind him of the options (basic refresh, full redesign, and phased approach), and recommend the phased approach because it balances cost and impact. Ask him to schedule a follow-up call next week. Professional but warm tone."

The more context you provide, the better the draft. Specifying the recipient, the background, the content, the recommendation, and the tone gives Copilot everything it needs.

Improving Emails You Have Already Written

You can also paste in an email you have drafted and ask Copilot to improve it:

> "Here is an email I wrote. Can you make it more concise and professional? [paste your email]"

Or:

> "This email sounds too aggressive. Can you soften the tone while keeping the same message? [paste your email]"

Handling Difficult Emails

Some emails are hard to write — delivering bad news, addressing a complaint, navigating a sensitive situation. Copilot is surprisingly good at these:

> "I need to email a client to let them know their project will be delivered two weeks late due to supply chain issues. I want to be honest and apologetic without making excuses. Offer a 10% discount on their next order as a goodwill gesture."

Copilot handles the delicate balance of honesty, accountability, and customer retention.

Professional Documents

Reports and Memos

For longer professional documents, give Copilot an outline of what you need:

> "Write a one-page memo to the leadership team summarizing last quarter's sales performance. Key points: total revenue was $2.4 million (up 12% from last year), our strongest product line was the Pro series (45% of revenue), customer retention improved to 87%, and our main challenge was slow growth in the enterprise segment. Include a brief recommendation section suggesting we hire a dedicated enterprise sales rep."

Proposals and Pitches

> "Draft a project proposal for implementing a new customer feedback system. We are a mid-sized e-commerce company with about 50,000 orders per month. The proposal should cover the problem (we currently have no systematic way to collect customer feedback), the proposed solution (implementing a post-purchase survey system), expected benefits, estimated timeline of three months, and rough budget of $25,000-$35,000."

Resumes and Cover Letters

Copilot is excellent at resume and cover letter writing because it can tailor the content to specific job postings:

> "Write a cover letter for a marketing coordinator position at Nike. Here is my background: five years of experience in digital marketing, strong skills in social media management and content creation, Bachelor's degree in Communications from Oregon State, previously worked at a small athletic apparel startup. Here is the job posting: [paste job posting]"

By providing both your background and the actual job posting, Copilot can highlight the most relevant parts of your experience and match the language and priorities of the employer.

Creative Writing

Copilot is not just for professional communication. It can also help with creative writing projects.

Getting Started with Creative Writing

If you are working on a story, poem, or creative project, Copilot can help you brainstorm, outline, and draft:

> "I want to write a short story about an elderly woman who discovers that her local library is closing. She decides to fight to keep it open. Give me a basic plot outline with five scenes."

Or:

> "Write the opening paragraph of a mystery novel set in a small coastal town in Maine during winter. Make the atmosphere eerie and the prose literary."

Overcoming Writer's Block

This is one of Copilot's most valuable creative applications. When you are stuck, try:

> "I am writing an essay about the importance of public libraries, and I have hit a wall after my second paragraph. Here is what I have so far: [paste your text]. Can you suggest three different ways I could continue from here?"

Copilot gives you options. You do not have to use any of them exactly – they are springboards to get your own ideas flowing again.

Poetry and Verse

> "Write a poem about the changing of seasons, focusing on the transition from autumn to winter. Use vivid imagery and a reflective tone. Free verse, about 16 lines."

You can then refine: "I love the imagery in the first stanza, but the ending feels too abrupt. Can you expand the final four lines?"

Editing and Refining Your Own Writing

One of the most practical uses of Copilot is improving text you have already written. This differs from having Copilot write from scratch — you start with your own words and use Copilot to polish them.

Grammar and Clarity

> "Edit this paragraph for grammar, clarity, and flow. Keep my voice and style, but fix any errors and make the writing cleaner: [paste your text]"

Tone Adjustment

> "Rewrite this email to sound more confident and assertive. Right now it sounds too apologetic: [paste your text]"

Simplification

> "This paragraph is too complex. Simplify the language so that a general audience can understand it without losing the key information: [paste your text]"

Structural Feedback

> "Here is the outline for my presentation. Does the flow make sense? Are there any gaps in the logic? Suggest improvements: [paste outline]"

Writing in Copilot for Word

If you have a Microsoft 365 subscription with Copilot, the writing experience gets better because Copilot works directly inside Word.

Drafting in Word

When you open a new Word document, you will see an option to "Draft with Copilot" (it usually appears as a prompt at the top of the blank document or via the Copilot button in the ribbon). Click it and describe what you want:

> "Write a two-page employee handbook section on our work-from-home policy. Include eligibility, equipment, expectations, and communication requirements."

Copilot generates the content directly in your document. You can keep it, discard it, or regenerate it.

Rewriting Sections

Select any text in your Word document and ask Copilot to rewrite it. Right-click or use the Copilot button and choose "Rewrite." Copilot offers alternative versions that you can accept, reject, or cycle through.

Summarizing Documents

Open a long document in Word and ask Copilot to summarize it:

> "Summarize this document in five key bullet points."

This is invaluable when you receive a long report and need to grasp the main points quickly.

Changing Tone Across a Document

> "Make this entire document sound more professional and less casual."

Copilot revises the language throughout.

Generating Content from References

If you have a reference document — meeting notes, research data — tell Copilot to use it:

> "Using the meeting notes in this document, draft a follow-up email summarizing the decisions made and the action items assigned."

Tips for Better Writing Results

After working with Copilot on writing tasks, the patterns that consistently produce the best results:

Give examples of what you like. If you have a sample of the style you want, share it:

> "Here is an example of the writing style I want: [paste example]. Now write a blog post about sustainable gardening in that same style."

Specify length. Copilot defaults to medium-length responses. If you want something specific, say so:

> "Write this in exactly 150 words." "Keep this under three paragraphs." "Make this a detailed, comprehensive guide of about 1,000 words."

Iterate aggressively. Your first prompt will rarely produce a perfect result. Plan on two or three follow-up messages to refine the output. This is normal and efficient.

Use Copilot for structure, then add your voice. A great workflow: have Copilot generate the structure and key points, then go through and add your personal touches, anecdotes, and voice. This pairs AI efficiency with human authenticity.

Do not accept the first draft blindly. Always read what Copilot produces. Watch for factual claims that need verification, language that does not sound like you, and sections that need more or less detail.

What Copilot Cannot Do (Yet) in Writing

A few honest limitations:

- **It does not know your personal voice.** It can mimic styles you describe, but it will not automatically sound like you. You will need to provide guidance and make edits.
- **It can produce generic content.** If your prompt is generic, the output will be too. The more specific and detailed your instructions, the more distinctive the result.
- **Long-form writing requires multiple rounds.** Copilot handles individual sections well, but writing an entire book or lengthy report in one prompt will not produce great results. Work section by section.
- **Creative writing can feel formulaic.** Copilot is good at competent creative writing, but truly original, distinctive literary prose still requires a human touch. Use it as a starting point, not a finishing point.

A Practical Workflow

A workflow many productive Copilot users follow for writing tasks:

1. **Start with Copilot.** Describe what you need and get a first draft.
2. **Evaluate.** Read the draft critically. What works? What does not?
3. **Refine with follow-ups.** Use two or three follow-up messages to adjust tone, length, detail, and structure.
4. **Copy and personalize.** Move the result into your final destination (email, document, website) and make personal adjustments.
5. **Proofread.** Give it a final read. You are responsible for everything that goes out under your name.

What You Will Learn Next

Writing is one side of the coin. The other is understanding the world around you — researching topics, learning new skills, and making sense of information. In Chapter 7, we explore how to use Copilot as a research and learning tool, turning it into your personal tutor, analyst, and fact-finder.

Chapter 7: Research and Learning

One of the most transformative ways to use Microsoft Copilot is as a research and learning tool. Traditional research means opening a dozen browser tabs, scanning articles, judging which sources are reliable, and piecing together an understanding from fragments. Copilot does not eliminate that process, but it makes it dramatically faster.

In this chapter, you will learn how to use Copilot to research topics, learn new skills, understand complex subjects, and verify what you read. Whether you are a student working on a paper, a professional staying current in your field, or just a curious person, these techniques will serve you well.

Copilot as a Research Assistant

Think of Copilot not as a search engine but as a research assistant. A search engine gives you links. A research assistant reads those links, synthesizes the information, and hands you a clear summary with the key points highlighted. That is what Copilot does when it combines its trained knowledge with real-time web search.

Here is a basic research workflow:

Step 1: Ask a Broad Question

Start with a general question to get an overview:

> "What is the current state of electric vehicle adoption in the United States? Give me an overview of market share, growth trends, and the major challenges."

Copilot will search the web, pull in recent data, and give you a synthesized overview with citations.

Step 2: Drill Down Into Specifics

Once you have the big picture, ask follow-ups to explore what interests you:

> "Tell me more about the charging infrastructure challenge. How many public charging stations are there, and how does that compare to what is needed?"

> "Which states are leading in EV adoption, and what policies are driving their success?"

> "What are the most common consumer objections to buying an electric vehicle?"

Step 3: Get Multiple Perspectives

Good research considers different viewpoints:

> "What do critics of rapid EV adoption argue? What are the strongest counterarguments to aggressive EV mandates?"

> "How does the environmental case for EVs look when you factor in battery manufacturing and electricity generation from fossil fuels?"

Step 4: Summarize and Organize

Once you have gathered enough information:

> "Based on our conversation, create a structured summary of the key findings about EV adoption in the US. Organize it by: current state, growth drivers, major challenges, and outlook for the next five years. Include the most important statistics."

This gives you a clean, organized document that captures your research.

Learning New Concepts

Copilot is an exceptionally patient teacher. Unlike a human tutor, it never gets frustrated, it can explain things in multiple ways, and it is available at two in the morning when you suddenly need to understand how the stock market works.

The "Explain It Simply" Approach

When you encounter a concept you do not understand, start with a simple explanation:

> "Explain compound interest like I am a complete beginner. Use a real-world example with specific numbers."

If the explanation is still too complex, say so:

> "That is still a little confusing. Can you break it down even further and use a more basic example?"

Copilot will adjust. Keep asking until it clicks.

The "Build Up My Understanding" Approach

For complex topics, ask Copilot to start simple and gradually increase complexity:

> "I want to understand how machine learning works. Start with the absolute basics — assume I know nothing about AI or programming — and then gradually build up to more technical concepts. Start with part one."

After Copilot gives you the first part:

> "That made sense. Give me part two, building on what you just explained."

This layered approach beats trying to understand everything at once.

The "Analogy" Approach

Analogies are powerful learning tools, and Copilot is good at generating them:

> "Explain how encryption works using an analogy from everyday life."
>
> "I do not understand the difference between a recession and a depression. Can you explain it using a simple analogy?"

If the first analogy does not resonate, ask for a different one:

> "That analogy does not quite click for me. Can you try a different comparison?"

The "Quiz Me" Approach

Active learning — testing yourself instead of passively reading — is one of the most effective study techniques. Copilot can help:

> "I have been studying the American Civil War. Quiz me on the major battles, key figures, and causes. Ask me one question at a time and tell me if I get it right."

Copilot will ask questions, evaluate your answers, and provide explanations when you get something wrong. This is surprisingly effective for studying.

Researching Products and Purchases

A major purchase — a car, a laptop, an appliance — usually means hours of research. Copilot compresses that work significantly.

The Comparison Approach

> "I am looking for a laptop for college. My budget is $800 to $1,200. I need it for writing papers, browsing the web, light photo editing, and occasional video calls. No gaming. Compare the top three options available right now with pros and cons for each."

The Decision Framework Approach

> "I am trying to decide between buying and leasing a car. My situation: I drive about 12,000 miles per year, I keep cars for about five years, and my budget is around $400 per month. Walk me through the financial comparison and tell me which option makes more sense."

The "What Should I Ask" Approach

When you are about to buy something and are not sure what factors to weigh:

> "I am buying my first home. What are the ten most important questions I should ask my real estate agent and what should I look for during a home inspection?"

This is incredibly useful: it surfaces the questions you did not know to ask.

Verifying Information: The Critical Skill

This is the most important section in the chapter. Copilot is a powerful research tool, but it is not infallible. Learning to verify is essential.

Check the Citations

When Copilot provides information grounded in web search, it includes numbered citations. Always click through to the sources, especially for:

- Statistics and specific numbers
- Claims about organizations, people, or policies
- Medical or legal information
- Financial data
- Anything you plan to rely on for an important decision

Cross-Reference Important Claims

For anything that matters, ask Copilot to find multiple sources:

> "You mentioned that the average cost of a wedding in the US is $35,000. Can you find two or three additional sources that confirm or contradict that number?"

Ask Copilot About Its Confidence

You can directly ask Copilot how confident it is:

> "How confident are you in this answer? Are there any aspects where the information might be outdated or uncertain?"

Copilot will often give you an honest read on where its knowledge is thin.

Watch for Hallucination Red Flags

"Hallucination" is when an AI generates information that sounds plausible but is simply not true. Warning signs:

- **Very specific statistics without citations.** If Copilot gives you a precise number like "42.7% of Americans..." but does not cite a source, be cautious.
- **Detailed claims about specific people.** AI models can sometimes confuse biographical details or attribute accomplishments to the wrong person.

- **Information about very recent events.** There is often a lag between when something happens and when Copilot's web search picks it up accurately.
- **Technical or scientific claims that seem too neat.** Real science is messy. If an explanation seems too clean, dig deeper.

The answer is not to distrust everything Copilot says — most of the time, it is accurate. The answer is to verify what matters.

Using Think Deeper for Complex Research

When research demands careful analysis rather than just finding facts, Think Deeper mode earns its keep:

> "I am considering investing in rental property versus index funds for retirement. Analyze both options considering: initial capital requirements, ongoing time commitment, historical returns, tax implications, risk profile, and liquidity. Use Think Deeper to work through this carefully."

Think Deeper takes longer but produces a more thorough, well-reasoned analysis than a quick response.

Research for Students

If you are a student, Copilot is a remarkable study aid — but you have to use it ethically.

What You Should Do

- **Use Copilot to understand concepts.** Ask it to explain topics you are studying.
- **Use it to find sources.** Ask Copilot to help you find relevant research papers, articles, and books on your topic.
- **Use it to quiz yourself.** Have Copilot test your knowledge before an exam.
- **Use it to check your reasoning.** Paste in your argument and ask, "Is my reasoning sound? What am I missing?"

- **Use it to brainstorm.** Generate ideas for papers and projects, then develop them yourself.
- **Use it to learn study techniques.** "What are the most effective ways to study for a biology exam?"

What You Should Not Do

- **Do not submit Copilot's output as your own work** unless your instructor specifically allows it. At most institutions, that is plagiarism.
- **Do not rely on Copilot for citations in academic papers** without verifying them. It can suggest sources, but you have to confirm they exist and actually say what Copilot claims.
- **Do not use it as a substitute for understanding.** Having Copilot write your essay teaches you nothing. Using Copilot to understand the material and then writing the essay yourself is learning.

Check your school's AI use policy. Policies vary widely, and the rules are your responsibility to know.

Research for Professionals

Professionals can use Copilot to stay current in their field, prepare for meetings, and make better decisions:

Industry Research

> "Give me an overview of the major trends in the healthcare industry for 2026. Focus on technology adoption, regulatory changes, and workforce challenges. Cite your sources."

Competitive Analysis

> "I work for a mid-sized accounting firm. What are the major cloud-based accounting platforms our clients are likely asking about? Compare QuickBooks Online, Xero, and FreshBooks in terms of features, pricing, and market position."

Meeting Preparation

> "I have a meeting tomorrow with a potential client in the manufacturing sector. Give me a quick briefing on the biggest

> challenges facing US manufacturers right now, including supply chain issues, labor shortages, and technology adoption."

Understanding Regulations

> "Explain the key provisions of the latest data privacy regulations in California. How do they affect small businesses that collect customer email addresses?"

For legal and regulatory questions, always verify with a qualified professional. Copilot is a starting point, not legal counsel.

Building a Personal Knowledge Base

A power technique: use Copilot conversations to build your own knowledge base.

After a productive research session, ask Copilot for a summary document:

> "Based on everything we discussed about renewable energy investment, create a comprehensive reference document I can save. Include key statistics, important distinctions, and practical decision factors. Format it with clear headings so I can scan it quickly later."

Copy it into a document or note-taking app. Over time, you build a personal library of well-organized research on topics that matter to you.

Using Pages for Research Projects

If you have access to Pages (available on paid plans), it is ideal for research projects. Instead of a chat that scrolls away, a Page gives you an editable canvas to organize findings, rearrange sections, and build a structured research document collaboratively with Copilot.

Start a research conversation in chat, then move the results to a Page when you are ready to organize and refine them.

Practical Research Exercises

Try these exercises to build your research skills with Copilot:

Exercise 1: Learn something new. Pick a topic you have always been curious about but never explored. Spend 15 minutes with Copilot. Start broad, then drill down into what interests you.

Exercise 2: Research a purchase. Use Copilot for your next significant purchase. Ask it to compare options, identify key decision factors, and present a recommendation.

Exercise 3: Verify a claim. Find a surprising statistic online. Ask Copilot to verify it and find supporting or contradicting evidence.

Exercise 4: Study a complex topic. Choose something you find confusing — the tax code, geopolitics, a scientific concept. Ask Copilot to explain it step by step using the "build up my understanding" approach.

What You Will Learn Next

Now that you can write and research with Copilot, it is time to broaden the scope. Chapter 8 covers everyday productivity — using Copilot for planning, organizing, problem-solving, and all the small tasks that fill your days. This is where Copilot stops being a tool you reach for occasionally and starts becoming a daily habit.

Chapter 8: Everyday Productivity

The previous chapters showed you how to use Copilot for writing and research — two of its most powerful applications. But Copilot is not just for big, structured tasks. It is also remarkably useful for the dozens of small decisions and organizational challenges that fill an ordinary day.

This chapter is about making Copilot a daily habit — something you reach for whenever you need to plan, organize, calculate, decide, or solve a problem. By the end, you will see Copilot less as a special-purpose tool and more as a general-purpose assistant that helps you move through your day.

Planning and Scheduling

Trip Planning

Copilot is an excellent travel planner. Instead of juggling a dozen travel websites, start with a conversation:

> "I am planning a five-day trip to Portugal in September for two people. We enjoy food, history, and beaches. Our budget is moderate — not backpacking, but not luxury either. Create a day-by-day itinerary with suggestions for where to stay, what to see, and where to eat."

Copilot generates a detailed itinerary. Then refine it:

> "We do not want to change cities every night. Can you revise this so we have two bases — Lisbon and the Algarve — and do day trips from each?"
>
> "What is the best way to get from Lisbon to the Algarve? Compare driving, train, and flying."
>
> "What should we pack for Portugal in September?"

Meal Planning

> "Create a weekly meal plan for a family of four. Two adults, one picky eight-year-old who only likes pasta and chicken, and one toddler. We

want healthy meals that can be prepared in 30 minutes or less on weeknights. Include a grocery list."

Follow up with:

> "My toddler is allergic to dairy. Can you adjust the plan and grocery list to eliminate all dairy?"

Event Planning

> "I am organizing a surprise 40th birthday party for my wife. Budget is $2,000, about 30 guests, and I need to do it within three weeks. She loves Italian food and live music. Give me a step-by-step planning checklist with a timeline."

Organization and Decision-Making

Organizing Your Life

Copilot can build systems and structures for organizing just about anything:

> "I am overwhelmed by clutter in my house. Give me a realistic, room-by-room decluttering plan that I can do over four weekends. Start with the areas that will have the biggest visual impact."

> "I have 200 unread emails in my inbox. Give me a strategy for getting to inbox zero and keeping it that way going forward."

Making Decisions

When you are stuck on a decision, Copilot can walk you through it systematically:

> "I have been offered a job in another city. Higher salary ($15,000 more) but I would have to relocate away from family. Help me create a decision framework — what factors should I weigh, and how should I think about this?"

> "I need to choose between three daycares for my daughter. Here are the key facts about each: [list details]. Help me compare them and identify which questions I should ask during my visits."

Copilot will not make the decision for you — nor should it. But it can organize your thinking, surface factors you might have missed, and clarify the trade-offs.

Creating Lists and Checklists

"Create a packing list for a week-long business trip to a cold climate. I have meetings every day and one formal dinner."

"What are all the things I need to do when moving to a new apartment? Give me a comprehensive checklist organized by timeline: one month before, two weeks before, one week before, moving day, and first week after."

"I am going camping for the first time. Create a complete gear and supply checklist for a two-night car camping trip in summer."

Math, Calculations, and Everyday Numbers

You do not need to be a math person to benefit from Copilot's facility with numbers:

Financial Calculations

"If I save $500 per month in a retirement account earning an average of 7% annually, how much will I have in 25 years?"

"I am comparing two job offers. Job A pays $85,000 with a 15-minute commute. Job B pays $95,000 but has a 50-minute commute. If I value my commute time at $30 per hour, which job is actually worth more?"

"Help me figure out how much house I can afford. My household income is $110,000, we have $40,000 saved for a down payment, and our monthly debt payments are $600."

Everyday Math

"I am splitting a restaurant bill between six people. The total is $247.83 before tip. We want to leave 20%. How much does each person owe?"

"I am remodeling my kitchen and need to tile a backsplash area that is 8 feet wide and 18 inches tall. The tiles are 4 inches square. How many tiles do I need, and how many extra should I buy for cuts and mistakes?"

"Convert this recipe from six servings to four servings: [paste recipe]."

Understanding Your Bills

> "Here are the line items on my electric bill: [paste details]. Can you explain what each charge means and tell me if anything looks unusual?"

Cooking and Recipes

Copilot is a surprisingly useful kitchen companion:

> "What can I make for dinner with chicken breast, broccoli, rice, soy sauce, and garlic? Give me two quick options."

> "I have a dinner party on Saturday and one guest is vegan, one is gluten-free, and one has a nut allergy. Suggest a three-course menu that accommodates everyone without making separate dishes for each person."

> "Give me a recipe for homemade pizza dough that is beginner-friendly. Include tips for someone who has never worked with yeast before."

> "I found a recipe that calls for tamarind paste, but I do not have any. What can I substitute?"

Health and Wellness

Copilot can be a useful wellness companion, with one important caveat: it is not a doctor, and it should never replace professional medical advice.

Fitness

> "Create a beginner-friendly workout plan for someone who has not exercised in years. Three days per week, no equipment, 30 minutes per session. Focus on building a sustainable habit rather than intensity."

> "I sit at a desk all day and my back hurts. What are some stretches I can do at my desk every hour?"

Understanding Health Information

> "My doctor said my LDL cholesterol is 145 and recommended lifestyle changes before considering medication. Explain what LDL cholesterol is, what that number means, and what lifestyle changes are most effective for lowering it."

"I am reading a medical report and I do not understand some of the terms. Can you explain these in plain language: [paste terms]?"

Important: Always discuss health information with your doctor. Copilot can help you understand medical concepts, but it cannot diagnose, recommend treatments, or replace a conversation with a healthcare professional.

Home and Car Maintenance

"My dishwasher is leaving a white film on my glasses. What are the most likely causes and how do I fix it?"

"My car's check engine light came on. I went to AutoZone and they said the code is P0420. What does that mean, how serious is it, and what should I expect to pay for the repair?"

"I want to paint my living room this weekend. I have never painted a room before. Give me a complete step-by-step guide, including what supplies to buy."

"What regular maintenance should I be doing on my home? Create a seasonal checklist for spring, summer, fall, and winter."

Personal Finance

"Explain the difference between a Roth IRA and a Traditional IRA. Which one makes more sense for someone who is 30, earns $75,000 per year, and expects to earn more in the future?"

"I have $8,000 in credit card debt across three cards. Here are the balances and interest rates: [list them]. What is the fastest way to pay them off?"

"Create a monthly budget template for a single person earning $4,500 per month after taxes. Include categories for all common expenses."

"I am thinking about refinancing my mortgage. Current rate is 5.5%, remaining balance is $280,000 with 22 years left. If I can get 4.2%, is it worth refinancing? What would I save?"

Image Generation with Microsoft Designer

Copilot includes image generation powered by OpenAI's GPT Image 1.5 (which began rolling out in January 2026, replacing DALL-E 3), with Microsoft Designer as a related editing surface. You can create images — social media graphics, birthday cards, logo concepts — simply by describing what you want. Image generation is available on both free and paid plans, though paid plans offer more generations per day and additional customization.

Chapter 15 covers image generation in depth: writing effective prompts, working with style options, iterating on results, and using Designer's full feature set. For now, know that it is there and remarkably easy to use: describe the image in the Copilot chat, and Designer creates it.

Using Copilot with Your Phone

The mobile app opens up some unique everyday uses:

Camera integration. Point your phone at something and ask Copilot about it: - Photograph a plant and ask, "What is this and how do I care for it?" - Photograph a menu in a foreign language and ask for a translation. - Snap a math problem from your kid's homework and ask for help solving it. - Photograph a product in a store and ask for reviews and price comparisons.

Voice conversations. Use the microphone to talk to Copilot hands-free — useful when you are cooking, driving (as a passenger, of course), or just prefer speaking.

Quick lookups. The mobile app is perfect for on-the-go questions: restaurant recommendations, directions, unit conversions, and more.

Creating Routines and Habits

One way to make Copilot a natural part of your day:

Morning. Ask for a briefing: "Give me a quick summary of the top news stories today" or "What is the weather forecast for today and this week?"

Work hours. Use Copilot for drafting emails, prepping for meetings, and answering questions that come up during the day.

Evening. Use Copilot for personal tasks: recipe ideas, homework help (yours or your kids'), weekend planning, or satisfying curiosity about something you heard or read.

As needed. Anytime you hit something confusing, face a decision, or want to save time on a task, open Copilot and ask.

The key is the habit of reaching for Copilot when you need help. The more you use it, the more natural it becomes, and the more time you save.

Practical Exercises

Exercise 1: Plan something. Use Copilot to plan your next weekend. Ask for activities based on your interests, weather, and budget.

Exercise 2: Solve a household problem. Think of something broken, messy, or inefficient in your home. Ask Copilot for a fix.

Exercise 3: Do some math. Work through a financial calculation you have been putting off — whether to refinance, how much to save for a goal, or how to split a complicated expense.

Exercise 4: Generate an image. Create one with Designer — describe what you want and see what Copilot produces. Chapter 15 goes deeper.

Exercise 5: Use your phone camera. Download the Copilot mobile app and use the camera to ask about something in the real world.

What You Will Learn Next

So far we have focused on personal and general-purpose uses. The next chapter shifts to the professional side — how Copilot transforms your work life when it is integrated into Microsoft 365. If you use Word, Excel, PowerPoint, Outlook, or Teams at work, Chapter 9 shows you how Copilot can make you meaningfully more productive.

Part III: Copilot at Work

"Productivity is never an accident. It is always the result of a commitment to excellence, intelligent planning, and focused effort."

— Paul J. Meyer

Chapter 9: Work and Professional Use

Everything we have covered so far works in any context – personal, academic, or professional. This chapter focuses on how Copilot transforms your work life once it is integrated into the Microsoft 365 tools that millions of professionals use every day. If your workplace runs on Word, Excel, PowerPoint, Outlook, and Teams, the rest of this chapter shows you how Copilot can make you substantially more productive.

We will walk through each major Microsoft 365 app and show you practical ways to use Copilot in real work. We will also cover meeting intelligence, organizational data access, and agentic capabilities that push Copilot beyond simple chat into genuine workplace transformation.

A note on what is ahead: This chapter is a preview. Chapters 10–14 go deep into each app – Word, Excel, PowerPoint, Outlook, and Teams each get their own chapter. The goal here is the big picture: a tour of the possibilities so you can see how the pieces fit before we dive into the details.

Before We Start: What You Need

To use Copilot inside Microsoft 365 apps at work, your organization needs one of the following:

- **Microsoft 365 Copilot for Business** ($18–21 per user per month, added to a Microsoft 365 business subscription)
- **Microsoft 365 Copilot Enterprise** ($30 per user per month, added to a Microsoft 365 enterprise subscription)

Your IT administrator controls the rollout, so if you do not see Copilot in your work apps, talk to IT.

If you are an individual on a paid Microsoft 365 plan (Personal, Family, or Premium), you will have Copilot in your apps as well, but without the organizational data features that business and enterprise plans provide.

Copilot in Word: Your Writing Amplifier

Copilot in Word goes beyond the standalone chat experience. It works inside your documents, with your content, in your workflow. You can draft entire documents from a description, rewrite selected text for tone or concision, summarize 40-page reports into five bullet points, turn meeting notes into formal summaries, and reference other files in your organization.

> "Draft a project status report for Q1 2026. Include a risks section and next steps."

> "Summarize this document in five key bullet points."

On business and enterprise plans, Copilot can pull from your SharePoint files and shared documents — a cross-file awareness that makes organizational Copilot fundamentally more powerful than standalone AI. Chapter 10 covers Copilot in Word in full.

Copilot in Excel: Making Sense of Your Data

If you work with spreadsheets, Copilot in Excel may change your work life more than any other feature. Instead of memorizing formula syntax, you describe what you need in plain English. Copilot analyzes your data, writes complex formulas, builds charts, flags patterns and outliers, and sorts or filters your spreadsheets — all from natural language.

> "Create a formula that calculates commission: 5% under $50K, 7% for $50-100K, 10% over $100K."

> "Create a bar chart comparing quarterly revenue by region."

The full walkthrough — including formula generation, data analysis, and visualization — is in Chapter 11.

Copilot in PowerPoint: Presentations in Minutes

Building presentations is one of the most time-consuming professional tasks. Copilot in PowerPoint can compress hours of work into minutes. It generates a complete slide deck from a text description, builds a presentation from an existing Word document, adds speaker notes, condenses a 25-slide deck to 15, and reorganizes slides into a more logical flow.

> "Create a 10-slide presentation about our new employee wellness program."

> "Turn this white paper into a 15-slide executive summary presentation."

Chapter 12 covers the full range of PowerPoint capabilities.

Copilot in Outlook: Email Under Control

Email overload is one of the biggest productivity killers in modern work. Copilot in Outlook attacks the problem head-on. It summarizes long threads, drafts replies in the right tone, prioritizes your inbox by urgency, and reviews outgoing messages for tone and clarity before you send.

> "Summarize this email thread. What was decided, and are there any action items for me?"

> "Draft a polite decline to this vendor's proposal. Leave the door open for future opportunities."

Chapter 13 walks through every Outlook scenario in detail.

Copilot in Teams: Meeting Intelligence

Copilot in Microsoft Teams is transformative for anyone who spends a significant chunk of their day in meetings. During meetings, it transcribes in real time, identifies who said what, and tracks topics and action items. After meetings, it generates clean summaries, lists action items with owners, and lets you catch up on meetings you missed — all from a single question.

> "I missed the marketing strategy meeting this morning. What were the key decisions? Are there any action items for me?"

Copilot also summarizes busy Teams chat channels, so you can catch up on hundreds of messages in seconds. Chapter 14 covers Teams in full.

Working Across Microsoft 365: The Graph Advantage

On business and enterprise plans, Copilot has access to the Microsoft 365 Graph — the layer that connects your organization's data across Microsoft 365. That means Copilot can draw connections across emails, files, chats, meetings, and contacts.

Practical examples:

> "Find all the documents related to the Anderson account that were shared in the last month." "What did our team discuss about the Q2 budget across emails and Teams chats?" "Who in our organization has expertise in data analytics?" "Summarize everything I need to know before my meeting with Jennifer Park tomorrow — pull from our recent emails, shared documents, and any relevant Teams discussions."

This cross-application intelligence is something no standalone AI chatbot can match. It is the deepest reason Copilot in Microsoft 365 is fundamentally different from a general-purpose AI tool.

Agentic Capabilities: Copilot Takes Action

One of the most significant developments in 2025 and 2026 is the emergence of agentic capabilities — Copilot taking actions on your behalf rather than just generating text.

Examples:

- Copilot can draft an email, create a meeting invitation, and add agenda items — all from a single natural language request
- It can monitor a SharePoint folder for new documents and summarize them automatically
- It can automate routine workflows — like sending a weekly status report compiled from data across multiple sources

Agentic capabilities are still expanding. The key shift: Copilot is moving from a tool you ask questions to a tool that executes tasks for you, with your approval and oversight.

Data Security and Privacy at Work

If you use Copilot at work, data security is a fair concern. Here is what you should know:

Your data stays within your organization. On business and enterprise plans, Copilot accesses your organizational data through the same security boundaries that already protect your Microsoft 365 environment. It can only see data that you have permission to access.

Microsoft does not train on your data. Your organization's data is not used to train the underlying AI models. Your confidential business information stays confidential.

Admin controls are robust. Your IT team can control which users have access to Copilot, what data sources it can draw from, and what actions it can take.

Conversations are logged. In enterprise environments, Copilot conversations may be subject to your organization's data retention and compliance policies. Check with IT if you have questions about how conversations are stored and managed.

Getting the Most Out of Copilot at Work

A few professional-specific tips that go beyond earlier chapters:

Use it for meeting prep. Before any important meeting, ask Copilot to brief you on the topic, summarize relevant documents, and suggest questions to ask.

Use it for status updates. Instead of spending 30 minutes on a weekly status update, tell Copilot what you accomplished and let it draft the report.

Use it for onboarding. New to a team or project? Ask Copilot to summarize the project's history, key documents, and recent decisions.

Use it to translate jargon. Got a technical document outside your expertise? Ask Copilot to explain it in terms you understand.

Use it to prepare for difficult conversations. "I need to give constructive feedback to a team member about missing deadlines. Help me plan what to say in a way that is direct but supportive."

Track your productivity gains. Notice how much time Copilot saves you each week. The data is useful for making the case to expand Copilot access at your organization.

Common Workplace Scenarios

A realistic workday with Copilot in the loop:

8:00 AM: You open Outlook and ask Copilot to summarize your overnight emails and flag anything urgent. Two minutes instead of 20.

8:30 AM: You join a Teams meeting. Copilot transcribes and tracks action items. Afterward, you get a clean summary in 30 seconds instead of spending 15 minutes writing up your notes.

10:00 AM: Your manager asks for a quick analysis of last quarter's sales data. You open the Excel file, ask Copilot to highlight the top trends and create a summary chart. Ten minutes instead of an hour.

11:00 AM: You need to respond to a complex client email. You ask Copilot to draft a response based on the thread, your internal pricing document, and last month's proposal. Five minutes of editing instead of 30 minutes of drafting.

2:00 PM: You need a presentation for a stakeholder update. You tell Copilot in PowerPoint to build a deck from your project status document. Twenty minutes of refinement instead of two hours of creation.

4:00 PM: A colleague asks you to review a 30-page contract. You open it in Word and ask Copilot to summarize the key terms, flag any unusual clauses, and identify the main obligations. Fifteen minutes instead of an hour.

That is a day where Copilot saved you three to four hours. Multiply across a week, a month, a year — the impact is significant.

Looking Forward

Microsoft is investing billions in Copilot, and the pace of improvement is rapid. Features that seem impressive today will be table stakes tomorrow. Agentic capabilities will expand, models will get more accurate, and the integration across Microsoft 365 will deepen.

The single best thing you can do right now is start using Copilot. The skills you build today — crafting effective prompts, iterating on results, knowing which tool fits which task — only become more valuable as the technology improves.

You now have a strong foundation for using Copilot across your professional work. In the chapters ahead we dive deeper into each Microsoft 365 app, explore advanced features like Pages, Think Deeper, and image generation, and cover specialized use cases that will push your Copilot skills further.

Chapter 10: Copilot in Word

If you spend any meaningful time writing — reports, proposals, memos, blog posts, anything — Copilot in Word is about to become your favorite feature in all of Microsoft 365. This is where Copilot stops feeling like a chatbot and starts feeling like a coworker who happens to be a very fast writer.

In this chapter, you will learn how to draft documents from scratch, rewrite existing text, summarize long documents, and get coaching on your writing. We close with a complete real-world workflow: creating a project proposal from start to finish.

How Copilot Shows Up in Word

Open a document in Word with a Microsoft 365 Copilot license and you will see Copilot in two places.

First, the Copilot button in the ribbon (Home tab). Click it to open the Copilot side panel, which works like a chat interface right inside your document. You can ask questions about the document, request summaries, or have a conversation about your content.

Second — the one most people miss at first — the inline Copilot prompt that appears when you are working in the document itself. In a blank document, a small Copilot icon labeled "Draft with Copilot" appears near the top of the page. In an existing document, place your cursor where you want new content and summon Copilot by clicking the icon in the left margin or pressing Alt+I on Windows.

The two entry points serve different purposes. The side panel handles conversation, analysis, and document-level tasks. The inline prompt generates and inserts content directly into your document.

Drafting Documents from Prompts

The most powerful feature in Copilot for Word is drafting. Describe what you want and Copilot generates a full document — or a section — in seconds.

To draft a new document, open a blank Word file and click the "Draft with Copilot" prompt. Then type your instructions. For example:

> Write a two-page project proposal for migrating our company's file storage from on-premises servers to SharePoint Online. Include sections for executive summary, current challenges, proposed solution, timeline, and estimated costs.

Copilot generates a complete draft from your prompt. The output will not be perfect — it never is — but it gives you a strong starting point.

Tips for better drafts:

Be specific about structure. Tell Copilot which sections you want, how long the document should be, and what format to use. "Write a report" gets you something generic. "Write a three-page report with an executive summary, three key findings, and a recommendation section" gets you something useful.

Name your audience. "Write this for a non-technical executive audience" produces very different output than "write this for the engineering team." Copilot adjusts vocabulary, detail level, and tone based on who will read it.

Reference other files. This is one of Copilot's strongest advantages over standalone AI. Reference files stored in your Microsoft 365 environment by typing "/" in the prompt and selecting a file. For example: "Draft a summary report based on /Q1 Sales Data.xlsx and /Customer Feedback Survey.docx." Copilot pulls information from those files and weaves it into your draft.

Specify tone. Words like "formal," "friendly," "persuasive," or "neutral" make a real difference. Without guidance, Copilot defaults to a fairly generic professional tone that may or may not match your needs.

After Copilot generates a draft, you get options to **Keep it**, **Regenerate**, or **Discard**. You can also refine the draft by typing more instructions in the prompt box — "Make the executive summary shorter," or "Add a section about risk mitigation."

Rewriting and Transforming Text

Drafting from scratch is great, but most of your time in Word is spent revising existing text. Copilot handles that well too.

To rewrite text, select the passage, then right-click and choose Copilot from the context menu, or click the Copilot icon that appears near your selection. You will see several options:

- **Rewrite:** Copilot generates alternative versions of the selected text. It typically offers three variations; you can pick one or discard them all.
- **Auto Rewrite:** Copilot rewrites with no additional input from you. Useful when you just want a fresh take on a paragraph.
- **Rewrite with instructions:** You tell Copilot how to change the text. "Make this more concise," "Simplify for a general audience," or "Make this sound more confident."

Rewriting shines in a few common scenarios:

Adjusting tone. You wrote an email in a hurry and it sounds too blunt. Select it, ask Copilot to "rewrite this in a warmer, more collaborative tone," and you get the same message without the edge.

Simplifying complex text. You pasted a paragraph from a technical spec into a report for stakeholders. Ask Copilot to "rewrite this so a non-technical reader can understand it."

Expanding bullet points. You have a list of brief notes and need full paragraphs. Select the bullets and ask Copilot to "expand each bullet point into a full paragraph with examples."

Condensing long passages. The opposite problem — you wrote too much. Select the section and ask Copilot to "reduce this to half its length while keeping all key points."

One important note: Copilot's rewrites are suggestions. They appear as alternatives you can accept or reject. Your original text stays put until you explicitly choose to replace it.

Summarizing Documents

If someone sends you a 30-page report and you need to understand it in five minutes, the Copilot side panel is your best friend.

Open the panel and try prompts like:

- "Summarize this document in five bullet points."
- "What are the three main arguments in this document?"
- "Give me a one-paragraph executive summary."
- "What decisions does this document recommend?"

Copilot reads the entire document and generates a summary tailored to your request. This works with documents you authored and documents others have shared with you, as long as they live in your Microsoft 365 environment (OneDrive or SharePoint).

You can also ask targeted questions about the content:

- "What does this document say about the project timeline?"
- "Are there any risks mentioned?"
- "What budget figures are included?"

These questions are grounded in the actual document, so the answers are usually accurate. Still, verify anything critical — Copilot can miss nuance or misread context, especially in documents with complex formatting or ambiguous language.

Summarization works best on well-structured documents. A disorganized source produces a disorganized summary. Garbage in, garbage out still applies, even with AI.

Coaching on Tone and Clarity

Copilot in Word includes a coaching feature that goes beyond simple rewriting. Instead of changing your text, it offers suggestions and explains why.

To access coaching, open the side panel and ask something like:

- "How can I improve the tone of this document?"
- "Review this document for clarity and suggest improvements."
- "Is this document persuasive enough for a board presentation?"

Copilot analyzes your writing and gives feedback. It might tell you the opening paragraph buries the lead, certain sections use too much jargon, or the conclusion never clearly states what you want the reader to do next.

This differs from rewriting because you stay in control. Copilot gives you the diagnosis; you decide how to treat it. For many writers, that is more valuable than automated rewrites — it sharpens your own skills over time.

Coaching is especially useful when you are writing for an audience you do not usually address: a technical person writing for executives, or a manager writing a company-wide announcement. Copilot flags language that might not land with your intended readers.

Working with Templates

Copilot integrates with Word's existing template system, and the two work well together.

Start with a Word template — say, your company's standard proposal template — and use Copilot to fill in the sections. Place your cursor in each section and use the inline prompt to generate content specific to that section.

You can also ask Copilot to follow a specific template structure even without a formal Word template. For example:

> Draft a project charter following this structure: Project Name, Project Sponsor, Objectives, Scope, Deliverables, Timeline, Budget, Risks, Approval Signatures.

Copilot generates a document with those exact sections, filled with placeholder content you can customize.

What Copilot in Word Cannot Do

A few honest limitations.

It does not know your company's specifics. Unless you reference particular files, Copilot generates plausible but generic content. It might invent project names, budget figures, or team members who do not exist.

It sometimes ignores formatting instructions. Ask for a bulleted list and get paragraphs, or ask for three sections and get five. This improves with each update, but it is not perfectly reliable.

It can be repetitive. Copilot-generated text sometimes circles back to the same point, especially in longer documents. Watch for this on review.

It does not replace editing. Every Copilot draft needs human review. Treat it as a first draft from a capable but uninformed assistant. The structure and language will be solid; the substance needs your expertise.

Real-World Workflow: Creating a Project Proposal

A realistic scenario from start to finish.

You are a project manager who needs to write a proposal for migrating your team from Slack to Microsoft Teams. Your manager wants a formal document by end of day. Here is how you would use Copilot to get there.

Step 1: Generate the First Draft

Open a new Word document. In the "Draft with Copilot" prompt, type:

> Write a formal project proposal for migrating our 200-person marketing department from Slack to Microsoft Teams. Include sections for Executive Summary, Business Case, Current State Assessment, Proposed Solution, Implementation Plan, Risk Analysis, Budget Estimate, and Conclusion. The tone should be professional and persuasive, aimed at senior leadership. Emphasize cost savings from consolidating communication tools and better integration with our existing Microsoft 365 environment.

Click Generate. In about 15 seconds, Copilot produces a multi-page document with all the requested sections. The content is generic — Copilot does not know your costs or team structure — but the framework is solid.

Click **Keep it** to insert the draft into your document.

Step 2: Refine with Referenced Files

Now make it specific. Suppose you have a spreadsheet with current Slack costs. Place your cursor in the Budget Estimate section, summon inline Copilot, and type:

> Rewrite this budget section using the data in /Slack Annual Costs 2025.xlsx. Compare current Slack costs to projected Microsoft Teams costs assuming we already have Microsoft 365 licenses.

Copilot pulls the actual numbers from your spreadsheet into the section.

Step 3: Rewrite the Executive Summary

The generated executive summary is okay but too long. Select it, click the Copilot icon, and choose "Rewrite with instructions":

> Condense this to three sentences. Lead with the cost savings number, then the integration benefit, then the recommendation.

Copilot produces a tight executive summary that gets straight to the point.

Step 4: Get Coaching on Tone

Open the Copilot side panel and type:

> Review this proposal for tone. Is it persuasive enough for a VP-level audience? Are there any sections that sound too technical or too casual?

Copilot analyzes the document and flags a couple of issues — maybe the Risk Analysis section sounds too negative, or the Implementation Plan leans on too much IT jargon. It suggests specific fixes you can make.

Step 5: Add a Missing Section

Your manager mentioned they want to see competitor analysis. Place your cursor after the Business Case section, summon inline Copilot, and type:

> Add a section called "Competitive Landscape" that briefly compares Microsoft Teams to Slack, Zoom Workplace, and Google Chat for enterprise use. Keep it objective but highlight Teams' strengths in Microsoft 365 integration.

Copilot inserts the new section in the right place.

Step 6: Final Summary Check

Before sending, use the side panel to ask:

> Summarize this document in five bullet points so I can use them in the email when I send this to my VP.

Copilot gives you a concise summary you can paste straight into your email.

Total time: about 20 minutes, for a document that would have taken two to three hours to write from scratch.

Key Takeaways

- Copilot in Word works through two entry points: the side panel for conversation and analysis, and the inline prompt for generating content directly in your document.
- Drafting works best when you are specific about structure, audience, and tone.
- Referencing other Microsoft 365 files with the "/" command lets Copilot ground its output in your actual data.
- Rewriting lets you adjust tone, length, complexity, and style without starting over.
- Summarization is ideal for quickly understanding long documents or extracting key points.
- Coaching helps you improve your writing rather than just replacing it.

- Every Copilot draft is a starting point, not a finished product. Plan to review and revise.

Chapter 11: Copilot in Excel

Excel is where Copilot might save you the most time — and where it demands the most patience. Spreadsheets are structured, precise, and unforgiving. A formula off by one cell reference can throw an entire report into chaos. Copilot brings natural language to that world, letting you describe what you want instead of remembering the exact syntax for XLOOKUP or SUMIFS.

In this chapter, you will learn how to analyze data, generate formulas, build charts, and work with Python in Excel. We close with a complete real-world workflow: analyzing a sales dataset from raw data to finished insights.

What You Need Before You Start

Copilot in Excel has one requirement that trips people up: **your data must be in a formatted table.** Not just data sitting in cells — an actual Excel table, created with Ctrl+T or via Insert > Table.

This is not optional. If your data is not in a table, Copilot will either refuse to work with it or prompt you to convert it. The reason is straightforward: tables have defined boundaries, headers, and structure that Copilot can read. A random collection of cells scattered across a sheet does not give Copilot enough context.

If you are working with existing spreadsheets, the first thing to do is convert your data ranges to tables. Select your data, press Ctrl+T, confirm the headers are correct, and you are ready to go.

How Copilot Shows Up in Excel

Like Word, Copilot in Excel appears in the ribbon and opens as a side panel. Click the Copilot button on the Home tab and the panel opens on the right.

Unlike Word, there is no inline Copilot prompt in Excel. Everything runs through the side panel. You type your request, and Copilot either modifies your spreadsheet directly or shows you a preview of what it plans to do.

When Copilot suggests a change — adding a formula column, creating a chart, sorting data — it shows a preview first. You can **Apply** the change, **Refine** your request, or **Discard** the suggestion. The preview step matters because spreadsheet changes cascade. Copilot respects that by never making changes without your approval.

Analyzing Data with Natural Language

This is the feature that makes non-Excel-experts fall in love with Copilot. Ask plain English questions about your data and Copilot answers.

Suppose you have a sales table with columns for Date, Region, Product, Units Sold, and Revenue. You can ask:

- "What was the total revenue last quarter?"
- "Which region had the highest sales?"
- "Show me the trend in units sold over the past 12 months."
- "What is the average revenue per transaction?"
- "Are there any outliers in this data?"

Copilot analyzes your table and responds with answers, often accompanied by small charts or highlighted data points. These responses appear in the side panel, not the spreadsheet, so they do not modify your data.

This is incredibly useful for quick analysis. Instead of building a pivot table to answer a simple question, you just ask. For deeper analysis you will still want pivot tables and proper reports, but for "I need an answer in 30 seconds" situations, Copilot is hard to beat.

Tips for Better Data Questions

Use column names. Copilot understands your table's column headers, so reference them. "What is the average of Revenue?" is clearer than "What is the average of the numbers?"

Specify time periods. "Total revenue for March 2026" beats "recent revenue." Copilot can interpret dates, but being explicit avoids ambiguity.

Ask follow-ups. After Copilot answers, you can keep going in the same session. "Break that down by region" or "Now show me just Q1" work well as continuations.

Generating Formulas and Functions

For many people, this is the killer feature. Describe what you want a formula to do, and Copilot writes it.

Open the Copilot panel and try prompts like:

- "Add a column that calculates profit margin as (Revenue - Cost) / Revenue."
- "Create a formula that shows the running total of Units Sold."
- "Add a column that categorizes revenue as 'High' if over 10,000, 'Medium' if between 5,000 and 10,000, and 'Low' if under 5,000."
- "Add a column that extracts the month name from the Date column."

Copilot generates the formula and shows a preview of the new column with sample results. If it looks right, click Apply and Copilot adds the column to your table.

This helps two kinds of people. First, those who know what they want but cannot remember the exact Excel syntax. If you know you need a nested IF but cannot recall whether the syntax is IF(condition, true, false) or something else, Copilot handles it. Second, those who do not know certain formulas exist at all. You may not know about TEXTSPLIT or UNIQUE, but you can describe what you want and Copilot reaches for the right function.

Complex Formulas

Copilot handles surprisingly complex formulas. You can ask for:

- **Conditional aggregations:** "Sum revenue only for rows where Region is 'West' and Product is 'Widget A'."
- **Lookups:** "Add a column that looks up the manager name from the Employees table based on the Employee ID in this table."

- **Date calculations:** "Add a column showing the number of business days between Order Date and Ship Date."
- **Text manipulation:** "Extract everything before the '@' symbol in the Email column."

When Copilot generates a formula, it usually explains what it does in plain English. This is good for learning — you see the formula, read the explanation, and build your Excel skills along the way.

When Formulas Go Wrong

Copilot's formulas are usually correct, but not always. Common issues:

- **Wrong cell references:** The formula points at the wrong column or uses an absolute reference where it should be relative.
- **Misunderstood conditions:** If your prompt is ambiguous, the formula filters on the wrong criteria.
- **Missing edge cases:** The formula may not handle blank cells, zeros, or error values correctly.

Always review the preview before applying. If something looks off, refine your prompt. "Add a column that calculates profit margin, handling cases where Revenue is zero by showing 'N/A'" beats hoping Copilot will catch the edge case on its own.

Creating Charts and Visualizations

Copilot creates charts directly from your data and does a decent job of picking appropriate types.

Try prompts like:

- "Create a bar chart showing total revenue by region."
- "Show a line chart of monthly sales trends."
- "Create a pie chart of market share by product category."
- "Make a chart comparing this year's revenue to last year's by quarter."

Copilot generates the chart and shows a preview. Apply it to insert the chart into your spreadsheet, then customize using Excel's native chart tools.

The charts Copilot creates are standard Excel charts, not special Copilot objects. Once inserted, you have full control — change colors, add data labels, modify axes, move it to a chart sheet. Copilot gets you 80% of the way there; you handle the final formatting.

Getting Better Charts

Specify the chart type if you have a preference. Copilot's guesses are reasonable, but if you want a stacked bar chart rather than a clustered one, say so.

Tell Copilot what to emphasize. "Create a chart that highlights the growth trend in the East region" produces a more focused visual than "chart the data."

Ask for multiple charts. You can request several in one session. "Create three charts: revenue by region, revenue by product, and monthly revenue trend" works well.

Python in Excel with Copilot

A newer feature that significantly expands what you can do in Excel. Python in Excel lets you run Python code directly inside your spreadsheet, and Copilot can write that code for you.

Why bother with Python in Excel? Because some analysis tasks are hard or impossible with standard Excel formulas. Statistical analysis, machine learning, advanced visualization, and complex data transformations are all areas where Python excels (no pun intended).

To use Python with Copilot, type prompts like:

- "Use Python to create a correlation matrix for all numeric columns."
- "Use Python to perform a linear regression on Revenue vs. Marketing Spend."
- "Use Python to create a heatmap of sales by region and month."
- "Use Python to identify clusters in this customer data."

Copilot generates the Python code, runs it in a secure cloud environment, and displays the results in your spreadsheet. The result might be a value, a DataFrame (a table-like output in your cells), or a visualization.

You do not need to know Python to use this feature — Copilot writes the code. But if you do know Python, you can review and modify what Copilot generates: click the cell containing the Python output to see the code in the formula bar.

Python Limitations to Know

- Python in Excel runs in a sandboxed cloud environment. It does not have access to your local machine's Python installation or any packages beyond what Microsoft provides.
- Available libraries include pandas, matplotlib, seaborn, scikit-learn, and several others. You cannot install arbitrary packages.
- Python calculations take a few seconds longer than standard formulas because they run in the cloud.
- The feature requires a Microsoft 365 subscription and may not be available on all plans.

Data Insights and Trend Identification

Beyond answering specific questions, Copilot can proactively identify patterns in your data.

Try prompts like:

- "What trends do you see in this data?"
- "Are there any anomalies or outliers?"
- "What are the key takeaways from this dataset?"
- "What factors most strongly correlate with high revenue?"

Copilot analyzes your data and presents findings, sometimes with supporting charts. This is useful for exploratory analysis — when you are not sure what questions to ask yet and want Copilot to surface what is interesting.

Treat these insights as starting points, not conclusions. Copilot identifies patterns, but it does not understand your business. A sales spike might come from a promotion you ran, a seasonal trend, or a data entry error. Copilot flags the spike; it cannot tell you which explanation is correct without more context.

Real-World Workflow: Analyzing a Sales Dataset

A complete scenario. You are a sales analyst and your manager wants a summary of Q1 2026 performance by end of day. You have a spreadsheet with 5,000 rows of transaction data.

Step 1: Prepare the Data

Open the spreadsheet. The data has columns: Date, Sales Rep, Region, Product Category, Units, Unit Price, and Revenue. Select all the data, press Ctrl+T to convert it to a table, and confirm the headers.

Step 2: Get a Quick Overview

Open Copilot and type:

> Give me a high-level overview of this sales data. What is the total revenue, number of transactions, and average transaction size?

Copilot calculates and presents the answers. You have the top-line numbers without writing a single formula.

Step 3: Break Down by Region

> Break down total revenue by region and tell me which region is performing best and worst.

Copilot provides the breakdown and may offer to create a chart. If so, apply it.

Step 4: Add Calculated Columns

> Add a column called "Quarter" that extracts the quarter from the Date column (Q1, Q2, etc.). Then add a column called "Revenue Category" that labels transactions over $5,000 as "Large," $1,000-$5,000 as "Medium," and under $1,000 as "Small."

Copilot generates the formulas and previews them. Apply both.

Step 5: Identify Trends

> What are the top 5 products by revenue? Has there been any change in the product mix compared to last quarter?

Copilot surfaces the top products and any notable shifts.

Step 6: Create Visualizations

> Create three charts: a bar chart of revenue by region, a line chart showing daily revenue trends for Q1, and a pie chart of revenue by product category.

Copilot generates each chart. Apply them to your spreadsheet.

Step 7: Advanced Analysis with Python

> Use Python to create a correlation matrix showing the relationship between Units, Unit Price, and Revenue across all regions.

Copilot writes the Python code, runs it, and produces a heatmap visualization in your spreadsheet.

Step 8: Generate a Summary

> Summarize the key findings from this data in five bullet points that I can paste into an email to my manager.

Copilot synthesizes everything you have explored into a clean summary.

Total time: about 25 minutes, for analysis that would typically take one to two hours of formula writing, pivot table building, and chart creation.

Key Takeaways

- Your data must be in a formatted Excel table (Ctrl+T) before Copilot can work with it.
- Ask natural language questions to get quick answers without building formulas.
- Copilot can generate formulas ranging from simple calculations to complex nested functions — always review the preview before applying.

- Charts are generated as standard Excel charts that you can customize after insertion.
- Python in Excel lets Copilot perform advanced analysis (statistics, machine learning, custom visualizations) that goes beyond traditional formulas.
- Copilot can identify trends and anomalies, but you need to apply your business context to interpret them correctly.
- Every change Copilot suggests goes through a preview step — nothing is applied without your approval.

Chapter 12: Copilot in PowerPoint

There is a particular dread that comes with opening a blank PowerPoint deck at 4 PM knowing you have to present at 9 AM tomorrow. You roughly know what you want to say, but the thought of building slide after slide — picking layouts, writing bullets, sourcing images, keeping it all consistent — is enough to make you consider calling in sick.

Copilot in PowerPoint does not eliminate the work of making a great presentation, but it eliminates the worst part: starting from nothing. You can go from a prompt or an existing document to a complete deck in under a minute. Then you spend your time refining instead of building.

In this chapter, you will learn how to create presentations from prompts and documents, add and format slides, generate images, and get design suggestions. We close with a real-world workflow: building a quarterly business review.

How Copilot Shows Up in PowerPoint

Copilot in PowerPoint works through the same side panel you have seen in Word and Excel. Click the Copilot button on the Home tab to open it.

A Copilot prompt also appears when you create a new blank presentation, similar to the "Draft with Copilot" prompt in Word. It invites you to describe the deck you want.

One difference from Word and Excel: Copilot in PowerPoint is more visual and structural. Instead of generating text or formulas, it generates entire slides — layouts, text, and sometimes images. The output is more impressive at first glance, but there is also more to review and adjust.

Creating Presentations from Prompts

The fastest way to build a deck is to describe what you want. Open a new presentation and type into the Copilot panel or the startup prompt. For example:

> Create a 10-slide presentation on the benefits of remote work for a company leadership audience. Include data points where relevant, use a professional tone, and end with a recommendation slide.

Copilot generates a complete deck with a title slide, content slides, and a closing slide. Each slide has a layout, title, body text, and sometimes placeholder images or icons.

What makes a good PowerPoint prompt:

Specify the slide count. Without guidance, Copilot tends to produce 8–12 slides. If you need exactly 6 or want a longer deck of 20, say so.

Name your audience. "For a board of directors" produces different content than "for a team meeting" or "for a customer presentation." Copilot adjusts formality, detail, and emphasis to match.

Describe the structure. If you have a specific flow in mind, lay it out: "Start with the problem, show three possible solutions, compare them in a table, and end with your recommendation." That gives you much more control over the narrative arc.

Mention design preferences. Copilot can incorporate themes and styles. "Use a clean, modern design" or "keep the color scheme minimal" gives it useful guidance, though it works within PowerPoint's available design options.

Once the deck is generated, click through to review. From here, you can ask Copilot to modify individual slides, add new ones, or restructure the deck.

Creating Presentations from Documents

This is one of Copilot's most practical features. Instead of describing a deck from scratch, point Copilot at an existing document and ask it to build slides from the content.

In the Copilot panel, type "/" to reference a file, then enter your prompt:

> Create a presentation based on /Q1 Business Review.docx. Focus on the key metrics and recommendations.

Copilot reads the document, identifies the key points, and structures them into slides. It uses actual content from your document — statistics, conclusions, recommendations — rather than generic filler.

This works with:

- **Word documents:** Reports, proposals, briefs, and memos translate well into slide decks.
- **PDFs:** Copilot can reference PDFs stored in OneDrive or SharePoint.
- **Other PowerPoint files:** You can use an existing deck as the basis for a new one.

Output quality tracks source quality. A well-structured report with clear headings and a logical flow produces a far better deck than a rambling document with no clear sections. If your source is messy, clean it up first or supplement the file reference with specific instructions about what to include.

Tips for Document-Based Presentations

Tell Copilot what to emphasize. "Focus on the financial results and skip the methodology section" prioritizes the right content.

Specify what to leave out. "Do not include the appendix or raw data" prevents slides full of detailed tables that belong in a handout, not on screen.

Set the slide count. "Create no more than 12 slides" keeps the deck focused. Without that constraint, a long document might produce a 25-slide deck that puts your audience to sleep.

Adding and Formatting Slides

After the initial deck, you will want to add, modify, or rearrange slides. Copilot handles all of this through the side panel.

Adding slides:

> Add a slide after slide 4 that shows a comparison table of Q1 vs Q2 metrics.

Add a slide with a timeline showing our product roadmap for the next 12 months.

Insert an agenda slide after the title slide.

Modifying existing slides:

Make slide 3 more concise — reduce the bullet points to three key items.

Rewrite the title of slide 7 to be more engaging.

Add speaker notes to slides 2 through 5.

Reorganizing:

Move the recommendation slide to the end of the deck.

Remove slides 8 and 9 — they are redundant.

These commands work well for incremental changes. For major restructuring, PowerPoint's Slide Sorter view alongside Copilot is often faster.

Generating Images for Slides

Copilot can generate images directly within your slides using its built-in image model (OpenAI's GPT Image 1.5, which began rolling out in January 2026 to replace DALL-E 3). You do not need to leave PowerPoint to find or create visuals.

To add an AI-generated image, ask Copilot:

Add an image to slide 3 that illustrates team collaboration in a modern office setting.

Generate an image for the title slide that shows a futuristic cityscape.

Copilot creates the image and places it on the slide. You can resize, reposition, or replace it using PowerPoint's normal image tools.

Keep in mind that AI-generated images have a particular look most viewers now recognize. For internal decks this is usually fine. For customer-facing or public presentations, you may want professional stock photos or your company's own imagery instead.

You can also use Designer (from the Design tab) to suggest layout improvements for slides that already have content. Designer analyzes your text and images and offers alternative layouts that often look more polished.

Design Suggestions and Layout

Beyond generating content, Copilot can help with the visual design of your deck.

Applying themes:

> Apply a professional, corporate design theme to this presentation.
>
> Change the color scheme to match our company colors (navy blue and white).

Improving layouts:

> Suggest a better layout for slide 5 — it has too much text.
>
> Convert the text on slide 6 into a SmartArt diagram.

Consistency checks:

> Review this deck for visual consistency. Are the fonts and colors uniform across all slides?

PowerPoint's Designer feature works alongside Copilot here. When you add content to a slide, Designer automatically suggests layout options in a panel on the right. Between Copilot's structural suggestions and Designer's visual ones, you can build a polished deck without any graphic design skills.

Speaker Notes and Presentation Prep

An overlooked feature: Copilot can generate speaker notes for your slides.

> Add detailed speaker notes to all slides. Each note should include talking points I can reference during the presentation, approximately 3-4 sentences per slide.

This is enormously helpful when you are building a deck someone else will present, or when you want a safety net during your own. The notes Copilot generates are reasonably good — they expand on the bullets without simply repeating them.

You can also use Copilot to prepare for questions:

> What questions might the audience ask after this presentation? Give me five likely questions and suggested answers.

What Copilot in PowerPoint Cannot Do

It does not create animations or complex transitions. Copilot adds content and suggests layouts, but slide animations, timed transitions, and build sequences are still manual.

It struggles with precise formatting. If you need a chart positioned exactly in the lower-right corner at specific dimensions, do that manually. Copilot gets you in the right ballpark; pixel-perfect control requires human hands.

It cannot embed live data. Copilot can create charts in your slides, but they are static. For a chart that updates when your Excel data changes, use PowerPoint's native Excel linking feature.

Design taste is subjective. Copilot's design choices are competent but generic. If your organization has brand guidelines, apply them manually or use a company template as your starting point.

Real-World Workflow: Building a Quarterly Business Review

You are a department head presenting your Q1 results to the executive team on Friday. You have a detailed Q1 report in Word and a data spreadsheet in Excel. Here is how to build the deck.

Step 1: Start from Your Report

Open a new PowerPoint presentation. In the Copilot panel, type:

> Create a 15-slide presentation based on /Q1 Department Review.docx. Structure it as follows: title slide, agenda, executive summary, key metrics (3-4 slides), accomplishments, challenges, team highlights, Q2 priorities, and closing slide. Keep the tone professional but confident. This is for an executive audience.

Copilot generates the deck, pulling actual metrics and findings from your report. Review the slides to confirm the key numbers are accurate.

Step 2: Add Data Visualizations

The metrics slides need charts. Open Copilot and type:

> On slide 4, add a bar chart comparing Q1 revenue to Q4 of last year. On slide 5, add a line chart showing monthly customer acquisition. Use the data from /Q1 Metrics Dashboard.xlsx.

Copilot creates the charts and places them on the right slides.

Step 3: Fix the Problem Slides

Slides 9 and 10 have too much text — Copilot dragged entire paragraphs out of your report. Ask:

> Condense slides 9 and 10 to no more than four bullet points each. Keep only the most important information.

Copilot tightens the slides.

Step 4: Add a Missing Slide

Your VP asked you to include a competitive landscape. Ask:

> Add a slide after slide 7 that shows a comparison table of our performance vs. two main competitors on these metrics: revenue growth, customer satisfaction, and market share. Use placeholder data that I can fill in.

Copilot creates a table slide with the right structure and placeholder values.

Step 5: Generate Speaker Notes

> Add speaker notes to all slides. For the metrics slides, include specific talking points about what drove the numbers. For the challenges slide, include how I plan to address each issue.

Copilot adds notes you can reference while presenting.

Step 6: Polish the Design

> Apply a clean, professional design theme. Make sure all slides use the same font and color scheme.

Copilot applies a consistent theme. From there, use Designer for additional layout suggestions on individual slides.

Step 7: Prepare for Q&A

> Based on this presentation, what are the five toughest questions the executive team might ask? Give me suggested responses for each.

Copilot analyzes the content and generates likely questions — on budget overruns, missed targets, competitive threats — along with suggested responses.

Total time: about 30 minutes, for a presentation that would typically take three to four hours from scratch.

Key Takeaways

- Copilot can create complete presentations from prompts or from existing documents — the document-based approach often produces better results because it uses your actual content.
- Specify slide count, audience, structure, and design preferences in your prompt for the best output.
- Use Copilot to add, modify, and reorganize slides incrementally after the initial generation.
- AI-generated images are convenient for internal decks but may not suit customer-facing presentations.

- Speaker notes generation is an underused feature that saves significant preparation time.
- Copilot-generated decks are strong starting points, but always review for accuracy, conciseness, and visual consistency before presenting.

Chapter 13: Copilot in Outlook

Email is the one productivity tool almost everyone uses and almost nobody enjoys. You open your inbox on Monday morning, see 87 unread messages, and feel your energy drain before your first sip of coffee. Half of those emails are 15-reply threads you need to catch up on. A quarter need responses you have been putting off because they need careful wording. The rest is noise to triage.

Copilot in Outlook attacks all of it. It summarizes long threads so you do not have to read every message, drafts replies so you do not start from a blank screen, coaches you on tone so your words land the way you intend, and helps you prioritize what actually needs your attention.

In this chapter, you will learn each of these features, and we walk through a real-world workflow: managing a busy inbox on a Monday morning.

How Copilot Shows Up in Outlook

Copilot shows up in Outlook in several places, depending on whether you are reading email, writing email, or managing your calendar.

When reading an email or thread, a Copilot summary card appears at the top of long conversations. For shorter messages, click the Copilot button in the ribbon to open the side panel and ask questions about the message.

When composing an email, a Copilot icon sits in the composition toolbar. Click it for drafting help, or highlight existing text for rewrite suggestions.

In the calendar view, Copilot can help you prepare for upcoming meetings by summarizing related emails and documents.

Copilot works in Outlook on the web (outlook.office.com), the new Outlook for Windows app, and Outlook for Mac. The classic Outlook desktop app has more limited Copilot integration, so if you are still on the older version, consider switching to the new Outlook for the full experience.

Summarizing Email Threads

This is the feature that will save you the most time, every single day. When you open a long email thread — the kind with 10, 15, or 20 replies going back and forth — Copilot summarizes the entire conversation in seconds.

For threads longer than a few messages, an automatic summary card often appears at the top of the thread. Something like:

> **Summary:** The team discussed the Q2 marketing budget. Sarah proposed a 15% increase, John raised concerns about ROI on digital spend, and the group agreed to revisit after the March metrics are in. No final decision was made.

The summary captures the essentials without making you scroll through every message. For a thread you have been cc'd on but have not been following, catch-up time drops from ten minutes to ten seconds.

For more detail or a different angle, open the Copilot panel and ask:

- "What decisions were made in this thread?"
- "What is being asked of me in this conversation?"
- "Summarize the key disagreements in this thread."
- "What action items came out of this email chain?"
- "What was the last thing agreed upon?"

Targeted questions extract exactly the information you need. "What is being asked of me?" is particularly useful — it cuts through the noise and tells you whether you actually need to do something or whether the thread is just informational.

When Summarization Works Best

Summarization excels with threaded discussions where multiple people are going back and forth. It handles meeting scheduling threads, project update chains, and decision-making discussions well.

It is less useful for single emails or very short threads, where reading the original is just as fast. It can also miss subtlety — if someone made a sarcastic comment or a politically delicate suggestion, Copilot may take it too literally or miss the subtext.

Drafting Emails

Starting an email from scratch always takes longer than it should, especially when the stakes are high. Copilot can draft emails from a description of what you want to say.

When composing a new email, click the Copilot icon in the toolbar and choose "Draft with Copilot." Then describe what you want:

> Write a follow-up email to the client thanking them for the meeting last Tuesday, summarizing the three action items we discussed, and proposing a check-in call next week.

Copilot generates a complete email draft. You can then:

- **Keep it** and send as is (though you should always read it first).
- **Regenerate** for a different version.
- **Adjust the tone** — options typically include Professional, Casual, Direct, and others.
- **Adjust the length** — shorter or longer.
- **Refine with custom instructions** — "Make the closing warmer" or "Add a sentence about the project timeline."

Drafting Replies

Replying is even easier because Copilot has the original message as context. When you click Reply, the Copilot icon appears in the composition toolbar. Click it, and Copilot suggests a reply based on the conversation.

For simple emails, the suggested reply may need only minor tweaks. For complex responses, give Copilot more direction:

> Draft a reply that politely declines the meeting invitation due to a scheduling conflict, but suggests two alternative times next week

> (Tuesday or Thursday afternoon). Keep the tone friendly and professional.
>
> Reply agreeing to the proposal but asking for clarification on the budget breakdown in section 3. Express enthusiasm about the partnership.

The key to good drafts is giving Copilot enough context about your intent. "Reply to this email" gets you something generic. "Reply agreeing but expressing concern about the timeline" gets you something you can actually send.

Referencing Other Content

Like Word, you can reference other Microsoft 365 files in your email drafts. Useful when you need to summarize something from another document:

> Draft an email to the project team summarizing the key points from /Project Status Update.docx and asking each person to confirm their deliverables by Friday.

Copilot reads the document and folds the relevant details into your email.

Coaching on Email Tone

One of Copilot's more nuanced features in Outlook is coaching. Instead of rewriting your email, it tells you how your message might be perceived.

After writing an email, click the Copilot icon and choose "Coaching by Copilot." Copilot analyzes your draft and offers suggestions in several areas:

Tone: Too formal? Too casual? Frustrated or passive-aggressive? Copilot flags language that might not land the way you intend.

Clarity: Are your requests clear? Will the recipient know what you are asking them to do? Copilot spots vague language and suggests making your asks more specific.

Sentiment: How will this email make the reader feel? Copilot flags messages that sound overly negative or that lack positive notes.

Reader impact: Copilot considers the overall impression and suggests adjustments.

Coaching is invaluable in a few specific situations:

- **Emotionally charged emails.** You are frustrated with a coworker and want your email firm but professional. Coaching catches phrases that come across as hostile.
- **Cross-cultural communication.** Emailing colleagues in a different country or culture? Coaching helps you avoid phrasing that might be misunderstood.
- **High-stakes correspondence.** An email to a client, a senior executive, or HR deserves extra scrutiny. Coaching is a second pair of eyes before you hit send.

Think of coaching as a trusted colleague reading your email and saying, "You might want to rephrase that second paragraph — it comes across a bit harsh." Except this colleague is available 24/7 and never tires of reviewing drafts.

Email Organization and Prioritization

Copilot can make sense of a crowded inbox by identifying what matters most.

Open the Copilot panel in your inbox and try:

- "What are my most important emails from today?"
- "Do I have any emails that require urgent action?"
- "Summarize what I missed while I was out last Thursday and Friday."
- "Are there any emails I have not responded to that might be time-sensitive?"

These queries triage your inbox fast, especially after a vacation or a day packed with meetings.

Copilot's prioritization weighs who sent the email (your manager ranks higher), whether you are directly addressed or just cc'd, and the content of the message (requests with deadlines outrank informational updates).

Calendar Assistance

Copilot's calendar features are not as extensive as its email features, but there are some useful ones.

Meeting preparation. Before a meeting, ask Copilot:

> Summarize all emails related to the Henderson project from the past two weeks so I can prepare for today's meeting.

Copilot gathers relevant threads and gives you a briefing.

Scheduling context. When you receive a meeting invitation, Copilot can provide context:

> What has been discussed in previous meetings with this group?

RSVP assistance. For meeting invitations that require a response, Copilot can help you draft acceptance or decline messages with appropriate context.

What Copilot in Outlook Cannot Do

It does not auto-sort or auto-file emails. Copilot can tell you what is important, but it does not move emails to folders or apply labels automatically. You still need rules and manual organization for that.

It does not handle attachments deeply. Copilot can reference documents in OneDrive or SharePoint, but it cannot analyze attachments embedded in emails the way it analyzes cloud-stored files.

It does not send emails for you. Every draft Copilot generates is a suggestion you review and send manually. There is no autopilot mode for email — and that is a good thing.

Sensitive content needs caution. If a thread contains confidential information, remember Copilot processes that content using Microsoft's AI services. Microsoft's commercial data protections apply, but use judgment about what you ask Copilot to process.

Real-World Workflow: Managing a Busy Monday Inbox

It is Monday morning. You took Friday as a personal day, and you have 94 unread emails. Here is how to get through them efficiently with Copilot.

Step 1: Get the Big Picture

Open the Copilot panel in your inbox and type:

> Summarize the most important emails I received on Friday and over the weekend. Highlight anything that requires action from me.

Copilot scans your recent unread emails and returns a prioritized summary. Something like: "Your VP requested the Q1 budget revision by Wednesday. The Henderson client responded to your proposal with questions about pricing. Three team members sent status updates with no action required."

Now you know what to tackle first.

Step 2: Catch Up on Key Threads

The Henderson client thread has 12 messages from Friday. Open it and read the Copilot summary at the top:

> The client is interested in the proposal but has concerns about the implementation timeline and pricing for phase 2. They asked for a revised timeline by Tuesday and requested a call to discuss pricing.

In 15 seconds, you know exactly where things stand. No need to read all 12 messages.

Step 3: Draft Your Priority Responses

The VP needs your budget revision. Click Reply, open Copilot, and type:

> Draft a reply confirming I will have the budget revision ready by Wednesday. Mention that I will include the updated headcount projections we discussed last week. Keep it brief and professional.

Copilot produces a clean, three-sentence reply. Review, tweak one phrase, and send.

For the Henderson client, you need a more careful response. Click Reply and tell Copilot:

> Draft a reply that acknowledges their timeline concerns, proposes moving the phase 2 start date back by two weeks, and suggests a call on Wednesday or Thursday to discuss pricing in detail. Be warm and reassuring — we want to keep this deal.

Copilot drafts the response. Use coaching to check the tone before sending.

Step 4: Coach Your Tricky Replies

You have an email from a colleague who missed a deadline, and you want to address it without damaging the relationship. Draft your response manually, then click Coaching.

Copilot reviews your draft and notes that the phrase "as I mentioned before" sounds frustrated and might put your colleague on the defensive. It suggests softening the language while keeping the message clear.

Step 5: Triage the Rest

For the remaining 80+ emails, ask Copilot:

> Which of my remaining unread emails are just FYI or informational and do not require a response?

Copilot identifies the status updates, newsletters, and automated notifications. Scan those quickly. The emails that need responses you now have time to address, because you handled the high-priority items first.

Step 6: Prepare for Your Afternoon Meeting

You have a project review meeting at 2 PM. Ask Copilot:

> Summarize all emails related to the Apex project from the past week so I can prepare for this afternoon's review meeting.

Copilot pulls together the relevant threads into a briefing you can review over lunch.

Total time to process 94 emails: about 35 minutes, versus the 90 minutes it would have taken to read and respond to everything manually.

Key Takeaways

- Thread summarization is Copilot's most valuable feature in Outlook — it turns 15-message threads into 3-sentence summaries.
- When drafting emails, give Copilot specific instructions about your intent, audience, and desired tone for the best results.
- Use coaching before sending high-stakes emails — it catches tone issues you might not notice yourself.
- Copilot can prioritize your inbox and identify what needs your attention, which is especially useful after time away.
- Reference Microsoft 365 files in your email drafts to include specific, accurate content from documents and spreadsheets.
- Always review Copilot's drafts before sending. It writes competent emails, but they are your emails once you hit send.

Chapter 14: Copilot in Teams

Microsoft Teams is where work happens in real time — meetings, chats, calls, and channel conversations. It is also where information gets lost. Someone said something important in last Tuesday's meeting and nobody wrote it down. A decision was made in a chat thread two weeks ago and now nobody can find it. Action items were assigned verbally, and half were forgotten by the time the meeting ended.

Copilot in Teams targets exactly these problems. It transcribes meetings, generates summaries, tracks action items, and helps you catch up on conversations you missed. If Copilot in Outlook saves you time on email, Copilot in Teams saves you time on everything else.

This chapter covers how to use Copilot during and after meetings, in chat conversations, and with channel agents. We will finish with a real-world workflow: running a productive meeting from start to finish.

Where Copilot Shows Up in Teams

Copilot is woven throughout the Teams experience in several places:

In meetings: During a live meeting, Copilot listens in real time and answers questions about what has been discussed. After the meeting, it provides a summary with key points, action items, and follow-ups.

In chat: For one-on-one and group chats, Copilot summarizes conversations, highlights key decisions, and helps you catch up on threads you have missed.

In channels: Copilot summarizes channel conversations and highlights important posts. Channel agents extend this further with automated workflows.

In the Copilot app within Teams: Open Copilot as a standalone app inside Teams and ask questions that span your entire Microsoft 365 environment — emails, files, chats, and calendar.

Copilot in Meetings: Before the Meeting

Copilot can help you prepare before a meeting starts.

If the meeting has an agenda attached, previous meeting notes, or related email threads, ask Copilot:

> What do I need to know before my 2 PM meeting with the product team?

Copilot pulls context from your calendar invitation, attached documents, relevant email threads, and previous meeting summaries (if you have had recurring meetings with the same group). It produces a briefing that might include:

- The meeting agenda
- Open action items from the last meeting
- Key topics discussed in related emails this week
- Documents that were recently shared with the meeting participants

This is the kind of preparation most people skip because it takes too long. With Copilot, it takes about 30 seconds.

Copilot in Meetings: During the Meeting

This is where Copilot earns its keep. During a live meeting, Copilot listens to the conversation (via transcription) and answers questions in real time.

Enabling Copilot in a Meeting

For Copilot to work during a meeting, transcription must be enabled. The meeting organizer can turn it on, or it may be on by default depending on your organization's settings. When transcription starts, participants are notified — a privacy requirement that cannot be disabled silently.

Once transcription is running, Copilot appears in the meeting toolbar. Click the Copilot icon to open its panel.

Real-Time Questions

During the meeting, you can ask Copilot questions without interrupting the conversation. These questions are private — only you see the answers. Useful when you zone out for a minute, get distracted by a Slack notification (it happens), or join late.

Try questions like:

- “What has been discussed so far?”
- “What did Sarah say about the budget?”
- “Has anyone mentioned the timeline for phase 2?”
- “What questions have been raised?”
- “Summarize the last 10 minutes.”

Copilot answers from the live transcription. You catch up on anything you missed without asking someone to repeat themselves.

Limitations During Live Meetings

Copilot’s real-time accuracy depends on transcription quality. Heavy accents, people talking over each other, or poor audio produce imperfect transcripts, and Copilot’s answers reflect those imperfections.

Copilot can only reference what was said in the current meeting. It does not have access to side conversations, private chats, or thoughts participants did not vocalize. If a decision was made through a nod and a thumbs-up, Copilot does not capture it.

Copilot in Meetings: After the Meeting

This is where most people get the most value. After a meeting ends (with transcription enabled), Copilot generates a summary that includes:

Recap: A narrative summary organized by topic. Not a transcript — a structured summary that captures the key points without the filler.

Action items: Copilot identifies tasks assigned during the meeting and attributes them to specific people. "John will send the revised proposal by Friday" shows up as an action item assigned to John.

Key decisions: When the group reaches a decision, Copilot highlights it. "The team decided to move forward with vendor B for the infrastructure upgrade" becomes a documented decision.

Follow-ups: Copilot flags topics that need further discussion or items deferred to a future meeting.

Accessing the Summary

After the meeting, open it in your Teams calendar and click the Recap tab. You will see the Copilot summary alongside the full transcript. You can also ask Copilot follow-up questions:

- "What did the group agree to regarding the launch date?"
- "Who is responsible for the next steps?"
- "Were there any disagreements during the meeting?"
- "What topics were not covered that were on the agenda?"

Sharing Meeting Notes

Share the summary with participants or with people who did not attend. Useful for stakeholders who could not make the meeting but need to stay informed.

Copy the summary to a Teams chat, email it through Outlook, or paste it into a document. Some organizations set up workflows that automatically post meeting summaries to a Teams channel for visibility.

Transcription and Intelligent Recap

Behind the scenes, Copilot's meeting features run on transcription and what Microsoft calls Intelligent Recap.

Transcription converts spoken words to text in real time. Teams identifies different speakers and labels them so you can see who said what. The transcript is available after the meeting in the Recap tab.

Intelligent Recap is the AI layer that analyzes the transcript and produces the structured summary, action items, and key decisions. It goes beyond transcription by understanding context — it knows the difference between "we should probably update the website" (a suggestion) and "I will update the website by Thursday" (an action item).

Transcription supports dozens of languages, and quality has improved sharply over the past two years. For meetings in a supported language with decent audio, transcription is highly accurate.

Chat Summarization

Teams chats can get long, especially group chats where people collaborate throughout the day. Coming back to 75 new messages and trying to figure out what happened is no one's idea of a good time.

Copilot in chat helps you catch up fast. In a chat, click the Copilot icon and ask:

- "What have I missed in this chat today?"
- "Summarize the key points from the last 24 hours."
- "Were any decisions made in this chat this week?"
- "What files were shared in this chat recently?"

Copilot reads through the messages and returns a structured summary. This works for both one-on-one chats and group chats.

You can also ask specific questions about past conversations:

- "Did anyone mention the Henderson project in this chat?"
- "What did the team decide about the new feature requirements?"
- "When is the next deadline mentioned in this chat?"

Chat summarization shines in group chats that serve as informal coordination channels. These chats bury important decisions between casual messages, status updates, and the occasional off-topic discussion. Copilot pulls the signal from the noise.

Channel Agents

Channels in Teams organize conversations by topic or project. Copilot can help you manage channels, but the more powerful feature is channel agents.

Channel agents are Copilot-powered bots added to a Teams channel to automate specific tasks. They can:

- **Answer questions from channel content.** Configure an agent to answer questions from documents and conversations in the channel. New team members can ask the agent for context instead of scrolling through months of history.
- **Surface relevant information.** An agent monitors the channel and highlights posts that meet certain criteria — flagging messages with deadlines or decisions, for example.
- **Automate routine tasks.** Set up agents to run standard workflows, like creating a task in Planner when someone posts a message in a specific format.

Set up channel agents through the Teams admin interface or Copilot Studio. Complexity ranges from simple (a Q&A bot based on channel content) to sophisticated (a multi-step agent that integrates with external systems).

For most users, the key thing to know is that channel agents exist and can save significant time for teams that live in channels. If your team has a channel where the same questions get asked repeatedly, or where important information gets buried in conversation flow, a channel agent can help.

The Copilot App in Teams

Beyond meetings, chats, and channels, you can open Copilot as a standalone app within Teams. This gives you the full Copilot experience without leaving Teams.

The Copilot app in Teams can:

- Search across your emails, files, chats, and calendar
- Summarize documents stored in SharePoint or OneDrive

- Draft content based on information from multiple sources
- Answer questions about your organization's shared knowledge

Useful when you need information that spans multiple sources. For example:

> What has the team discussed about the Apex project in the last two weeks? Check emails, chats, and meeting transcripts.

Copilot aggregates information from across your Microsoft 365 environment and presents a unified summary. Cross-app search is one of Copilot's genuine advantages over standalone AI tools that lack access to your organizational data.

What Copilot in Teams Cannot Do

It requires transcription for meeting features. Without transcription, Copilot cannot summarize meetings or track action items. Some organizations disable transcription for compliance or privacy reasons, which effectively turns off Copilot's meeting features.

It does not join external meetings automatically. If you are in a meeting hosted by someone outside your organization, Copilot may be unavailable depending on the host's settings.

Action items are suggestions, not commitments. Copilot identifies what it thinks are action items, but it does not create tasks in Planner or To Do automatically (unless an agent is configured to do so). The people involved still have to follow through.

It cannot read the room. Copilot captures words, not tone, body language, or political dynamics. A summary might miss that half the team looked skeptical during the proposal, or that the VP's silence on a topic was itself a statement.

Real-World Workflow: Running a Productive Meeting

You are leading a weekly project status meeting with eight team members. Here is how to make it the most productive meeting of the week.

Before the Meeting

Open Copilot in Teams and type:

> Prepare me for today's 10 AM project sync. What were the action items from last week's meeting, and have any of them been discussed in chat or email since then?

Copilot pulls last week's action items and checks whether team members have followed up. You know who completed their tasks and who needs a nudge.

Starting the Meeting

When the meeting starts, confirm transcription is enabled (it should be by default for recurring meetings if your admin has configured it). Copilot appears in the meeting toolbar.

During the Meeting

As the discussion progresses, you are facilitating and cannot take detailed notes. Fine — Copilot is capturing everything.

Midway through, a team member references a decision from three weeks ago you do not remember. Without interrupting the flow, you ask Copilot privately:

> What did we decide about the API integration approach in our meeting on March 10th?

Copilot checks the previous meeting's transcript and answers. You stay informed without derailing the current conversation.

Near the end, someone proposes changing the project timeline. You want the implications understood before the meeting ends:

> What action items have been discussed so far in this meeting?

Copilot lists the action items it has identified. You read them aloud: "Before we wrap up, let me confirm the action items..." Everyone leaves aligned.

After the Meeting

Within minutes of the meeting ending, Copilot generates the Intelligent Recap. Review it in the Recap tab. The summary includes:

- Four key topics discussed
- Six action items with names and deadlines
- Two decisions made
- One topic deferred to next week

Copy the summary and paste it into the project's Teams channel:

> Here are the notes from today's sync: [paste Copilot summary]

Team members who missed the meeting know exactly what happened. Those who attended have a clear record of their commitments.

Following Up

Two days later, you want to check on progress. Open Copilot in Teams and ask:

> Have any of the action items from Monday's project sync been discussed in our team chat or email since the meeting?

Copilot checks the relevant conversations and reports that three of six items have been mentioned, with one marked complete. You follow up with the team members who have not reported progress.

Total time on meeting management: about 15 minutes across the week, compared to the hour or more it typically takes to prepare agendas, take notes, distribute minutes, and chase action items.

Key Takeaways

- Copilot in Teams requires transcription to be enabled for meeting features — make sure your organization allows it.
- Real-time questions during meetings let you catch up privately without disrupting the conversation.

- Meeting summaries with action items, decisions, and follow-ups replace the need for manual note-taking.
- Chat summarization helps you catch up on group conversations without reading every message.
- Channel agents can automate routine tasks and answer questions based on channel content.
- The Copilot app in Teams searches across your entire Microsoft 365 environment — emails, files, chats, and meetings.
- Copilot captures words, not context. Always review summaries for accuracy and completeness before sharing them as official meeting notes.

Part IV: Advanced Features

"The most dangerous phrase in the language is, 'We have always done it this way.'"

— Grace Hopper

Chapter 15: Image Generation with Designer

Until recently, if you needed a custom image — for a presentation, a social media post, a blog, or an internal document — you had three options: hire a designer, use a stock photo, or spend an hour fumbling with Canva. Copilot adds a fourth: describe the image you want, and AI creates it.

Microsoft Copilot's image generation is now powered by OpenAI's GPT Image 1.5, which began rolling out in January 2026 as the successor to DALL-E 3. (DALL-E 3 itself is being deprecated in May 2026.) Microsoft Designer is a related but separate creative surface — still transitioning across the underlying model — where you can build social posts, flyers, and templated graphics around the images Copilot generates. You can create images directly from the Copilot chat interface or open Designer for more layout control. Results range from surprisingly good to occasionally bizarre, and knowing how to prompt effectively makes the difference.

This chapter covers how to create images from text descriptions, edit and iterate on results, work with style options, and identify practical use cases. We will close with a walkthrough: creating a social media graphic from scratch.

How Image Generation Works in Copilot

You can generate images in several places:

In the Copilot chat (at copilot.microsoft.com, the Copilot app, or the Edge sidebar): Ask Copilot to create an image. Type something like "Create an image of a mountain landscape at sunset" and Copilot generates the image right in the conversation.

In Microsoft Designer (designer.microsoft.com): Microsoft's dedicated design tool offers more control over image generation, editing, and templates. Create images from text prompts and drop them into pre-designed templates for social media, presentations, flyers, and more.

In PowerPoint: As covered in Chapter 12, Copilot can generate images directly within your slides.

In Word: Copilot can also generate images to include in documents, though this is less common than presentations.

When you submit an image prompt, Copilot sends it to GPT Image 1.5, which generates one or more images based on your description. The images are original creations — not pulled from a stock photo library or assembled from existing images. Each one is generated from scratch based on the patterns the model learned during training.

Creating Images from Text Descriptions

The quality of your image depends almost entirely on how you describe what you want. Vague prompts produce vague results. Specific prompts produce specific results. Here is how to write better ones.

Start with the Subject

What is the main thing in the image? Be concrete.

- Weak: "A person working"
- Better: "A woman in her 30s sitting at a modern desk with a laptop, wearing business casual clothing"

Add the Setting

Where does this scene take place?

- Weak: "In an office"
- Better: "In a bright, open-plan office with floor-to-ceiling windows and plants on the windowsill"

Specify the Style

What should the image look like? Photorealistic? Illustration? Watercolor? Flat design?

- "Photorealistic photograph"
- "Minimalist flat illustration"
- "Watercolor painting style"
- "3D render"
- "Pencil sketch"

Include Lighting and Mood

These details dramatically affect the result.

- "Warm golden hour lighting"
- "Bright, even studio lighting"
- "Dramatic shadows with a single light source"
- "Soft, dreamy lighting with pastel tones"

Describe the Composition

How should the image be framed?

- "Close-up portrait"
- "Wide-angle landscape shot"
- "Top-down flat lay"
- "Isometric view"

A Complete Example

Putting it all together:

> Create a photorealistic image of a diverse team of four people having a productive meeting in a modern glass-walled conference room. They are looking at a presentation on a large screen. The lighting is bright and natural, coming from large windows. The mood is collaborative and energetic. Shot from a slightly elevated angle.

That gives the image model enough detail to produce a focused, professional result.

Editing and Iterating on Images

Your first result will rarely be exactly what you want. Copilot makes iteration easy.

After an image is generated, you can:

Ask for modifications in the conversation:

- "Make the background lighter."
- "Remove the text in the image."
- "Change the woman's shirt to blue."
- "Make this more minimalist."
- "Add a coffee cup to the desk."

Copilot generates a new version based on your modifications. Each iteration is a fresh generation — Copilot does not edit the pixels of the existing image; it creates a new one incorporating your feedback.

Request variations:

- "Give me three more versions of this image."
- "Show me the same scene but in a different art style."
- "Create a version of this with a warmer color palette."

Start over with adjusted prompts:

If the image is heading in the wrong direction, rewrite your prompt entirely rather than trying to patch individual details. A fresh start with a better description is often faster than iterating on a flawed image.

Working in Designer

Microsoft Designer offers more sophisticated editing tools than Copilot chat. In Designer, you can:

- **Remove backgrounds** from generated images.
- **Add text overlays** with professional typography.
- **Place images into templates** — social media posts, flyers, invitations, and more.

- **Adjust colors, filters, and effects** with visual controls.
- **Resize images** for different platforms (Instagram square, Facebook cover, LinkedIn post, etc.).

For professional use, generate the base image in Copilot chat and polish it in Designer. That is usually the most efficient workflow.

Style Options

Copilot's image model can produce images in a wide range of styles. Effective style keywords for your prompts:

Photographic styles: - Professional headshot - Editorial photography - Product photography on white background - Documentary/candid style - Aerial/drone photography

Illustration styles: - Flat vector illustration - Hand-drawn sketch - Watercolor painting - Digital art - Pixel art - Comic book style - Infographic style

Design styles: - Minimalist - Retro/vintage - Corporate/professional - Whimsical - Abstract geometric

Artistic references: - Art deco - Mid-century modern - Impressionist - Pop art

Mixing styles produces interesting results. "A watercolor illustration of a cityscape in the style of art deco" is a valid prompt that produces distinctive output.

Image Generation Limits and Boosts

Image generation is not unlimited. Microsoft uses a system of "boosts" to manage usage.

What are boosts? Each image generation uses one or more boosts. When you run out, you can still generate images, but they go into a queue rather than running immediately.

How many boosts do you get? Varies by plan:

- **Free Copilot users:** A limited number of daily boosts (the exact number changes, but it is typically around 15).
- **Paid Microsoft 365 consumer subscribers (Personal, Family, Premium):** Substantially higher daily boost allowances than Free, with Premium offering the most generous limits. Microsoft does not publish the exact per-tier daily caps.
- **Microsoft 365 Copilot for Business/Enterprise:** Boosts are included as part of the license.

When do boosts reset? Daily, though the exact reset time depends on your region.

What happens when you run out? Images still generate, just slower. Instead of appearing in seconds, they might take a minute or more. Quality is the same — only speed changes.

For most casual users, the daily allocation is sufficient. If you are generating large volumes (for a marketing campaign or a content library), you may hit the limit and need to spread the work across multiple days.

Practical Use Cases

Be honest about what AI image generation is good for and where it falls short.

Where It Works Well

Social media content. Blog post headers, social graphics, and promotional images are a great fit. The images need to be eye-catching and relevant, not photographically accurate.

Presentations. Custom illustrations for slides beat generic stock photos because they match your specific content. A "team collaboration" presentation with a custom illustration looks more intentional than one with a stock photo everyone has seen a hundred times.

Concept visualization. When you are describing a future product, an event layout, or a design concept, AI-generated images communicate your vision before anything is built.

Internal documents. Reports, newsletters, and internal communications benefit from visual variety. AI images add polish without the cost of custom photography or illustration.

Brainstorming. When you are exploring visual directions — "What would our brand look like in a retro style?" — image generation lets you experiment fast.

Where It Falls Short

Text in images. AI image models still struggle with text. They misspell words, distort letters, and place text in awkward positions. If you need text in your image, generate without it and add text later in Designer or another tool.

Precise brand assets. If you need an image that exactly matches your brand guidelines — specific hex colors, logo placement, precise typography — AI generation is not reliable enough. Use it for concept exploration, then hand the direction to a designer.

Photographs of real people or products. AI "photos" of people can look uncanny, and renders of existing products may not be accurate. For product photography, use actual photographs.

Legal and compliance contexts. Do not use AI-generated images where photographic evidence is required (insurance claims, legal documents, etc.). They are fabrications, not documentation.

Sensitive subjects. Copilot's image model has content filters that block violent, explicit, or harmful content. It also restricts generating images of real, identifiable people.

Content Policies and Ethical Considerations

Microsoft applies content policies to image generation. You cannot generate:

- Images of real, named individuals

- Violent or graphic content
- Explicit or adult content
- Content that promotes hate or discrimination
- Misleading content designed to look like real photographs for deceptive purposes

Restrictions are enforced automatically. If your prompt trips a filter, Copilot declines and may suggest an alternative.

AI-generated images should also be used transparently. If you publish one, disclose it — good practice generally, and in some contexts a legal requirement. Microsoft adds invisible metadata to Copilot-generated images flagging them as AI-created, but visible disclosure is still recommended for public-facing content.

Walkthrough: Creating a Social Media Graphic

You are a marketing coordinator and need a graphic for a LinkedIn post announcing your company's new sustainability initiative. Here is how to create it.

Step 1: Generate the Base Image

Open Copilot and type:

> Create a modern, professional illustration of a green city with renewable energy elements — solar panels, wind turbines, electric vehicles, and green rooftops. Use a clean, flat illustration style with a bright, optimistic color palette of greens, blues, and whites. The composition should be a wide landscape format suitable for a LinkedIn post.

Copilot generates the image. Review it — is the mood right? Are the elements present?

Step 2: Iterate

The first result is close but the colors are too dark. Ask:

> Make the color palette brighter and more vibrant. Add more white space so there is room to overlay text.

Copilot generates a revised version with a lighter, more open composition.

Step 3: Polish in Designer

Open Microsoft Designer and upload or open the image you generated. From here:

- Choose a LinkedIn post template.
- Place your image as the background.
- Add a text overlay: "Building a Greener Future — Our 2026 Sustainability Commitment."
- Adjust the text color for readability against the illustration.
- Add your company logo in the corner.

Step 4: Resize for Other Platforms

In Designer, resize the graphic for Instagram (square), X (16:9), and your website banner (wide format). Designer adjusts the layout while keeping key elements visible.

Step 5: Download and Post

Export the final graphics in the appropriate formats and post them to your social channels.

Total time: about 15 minutes, versus one to two hours of searching for stock photos, negotiating with a designer, or wrestling with Canva templates.

Key Takeaways

- Copilot generates images using OpenAI's GPT Image 1.5 (rolling out since January 2026, succeeding DALL-E 3) through the Copilot chat interface, with Microsoft Designer as a related editing surface.
- Detailed prompts produce dramatically better results — specify subject, setting, style, lighting, and composition.

- Iterate on images by requesting modifications, variations, or starting fresh with a better prompt.
- Designer adds text, templates, background removal, and resizing tools on top of basic image generation.
- Image generation works well for social media, presentations, concept visualization, and internal documents — it is less suited for precise brand assets or photographs of real subjects.
- Text in AI-generated images is unreliable — add text afterward using Designer or another tool.
- Be aware of content policies and ethical considerations, especially when publishing AI-generated images publicly.

Chapter 16: Copilot Pages and Notebooks

Up to this point, every interaction you have had with Copilot has followed the same pattern: you type a prompt, Copilot responds, and the conversation scrolls downward into the chat history. It works, but chat is linear. You cannot easily reorganize a response, expand one section while leaving others alone, or share a specific part of the conversation with a colleague who can then build on it.

Pages and Notebooks change this. They move Copilot's output out of the chat window and into workspaces where you can edit, organize, collaborate, and build on AI-generated content. Think of them as the bridge between having a conversation with AI and actually producing something useful from it.

This chapter covers what Pages and Notebooks are, how they differ from each other and from standard chat, how to create and share them, and how to use their collaboration features. We will finish with a real-world workflow: building a collaborative research document with your team.

What Are Copilot Pages?

Pages are a collaborative AI canvas. When Copilot generates a response in chat that you want to work with more seriously — edit, share, or expand — send it to a Page.

A Page looks like a lightweight document. It has a clean editing surface where you can add text, format content, and restructure information. Unlike a Word document, a Page stays connected to Copilot. Ask Copilot to add content, rewrite sections, or generate new material — all within the Page.

Here is the key differentiator: Pages are collaborative. Share a Page with other people and they can edit alongside you, much like a shared Google Doc or a co-authored Word document. Everyone on the Page also has access to Copilot, so multiple people can use AI to contribute to the same document simultaneously.

Creating a Page

Two main ways to create a Page:

From a chat response: When Copilot generates a response you want to develop further, look for the "Edit in Pages" button (or similar option) below the response. Click it, and the response opens in a new Page where you can edit, expand, and share.

From scratch: In the Copilot app (copilot.microsoft.com or the Copilot app in Teams), create a new Page directly. Start with a prompt, and instead of keeping the output in chat, direct it to a Page.

What You Can Do in a Page

Once you are in a Page, you have several tools available:

Direct editing: Click anywhere in the text and type. Add, delete, and modify content like any editor. This is the fundamental difference from chat — you are not stuck with Copilot's exact output.

Copilot assistance: Ask Copilot to add content, rewrite sections, or answer follow-up questions. The AI-generated content appears in the Page, where you can edit it immediately.

Formatting: Pages support headings, bullet points, numbered lists, tables, and basic formatting. Less full-featured than Word, but enough for most working documents.

Sharing: Share the Page with specific people in your organization. They get a link and can view or edit depending on the permissions you set.

Real-time collaboration: When multiple people have edit access, they can work on the Page simultaneously. Each person can also invoke Copilot independently — one person might ask Copilot to expand the introduction while another asks for a comparison table.

What Are Copilot Notebooks?

Notebooks serve a different purpose. Pages are about collaboration and lightweight editing; Notebooks are built for long-form content generation — situations where you need Copilot to produce substantial output that exceeds what fits comfortably in a chat response.

Standard Copilot chat caps response length. Ask Copilot to "write a 5,000-word report" and the chat response typically taps out well short of 5,000 words. Notebooks remove this constraint. They give Copilot more room to generate longer, more detailed content.

When to Use a Notebook

Use a Notebook when:

- You need long-form content: comprehensive reports, detailed analyses, extended guides, or thorough explanations.
- You want to provide a longer, more detailed prompt without the constraints of the chat input box.
- You need to generate content that will serve as a starting point for a longer document (which you might then move to Word for final formatting).

How Notebooks Work

Open a Notebook from the Copilot interface (look for the Notebook option in the app menu or conversation toolbar). You will see a split view:

The prompt area: A large text input where you can write detailed prompts. Unlike chat, where you type a sentence or two, the Notebook prompt area invites longer, more detailed instructions.

The output area: Copilot generates its response here. The area supports longer output than standard chat, and you can edit the output directly.

Example. In the prompt area, you write:

> Write a comprehensive guide to onboarding new employees at a mid-size technology company. Include sections on: pre-arrival preparation,

first day activities, first week goals, 30–60–90 day milestones, buddy and mentor programs, tools and systems setup, cultural integration, and measuring onboarding success. Each section should be 400–600 words with specific, actionable recommendations. The audience is HR managers who are building or improving their onboarding process.

Copilot generates a detailed, multi-section document in the output area. Edit it directly, ask Copilot to revise specific sections, or copy the content to Word for final polishing.

Pages vs. Notebooks vs. Standard Chat

Knowing when to use each format saves time and frustration.

Standard Chat

Best for: Quick questions, short tasks, brainstorming, getting a fast answer.

Limitations: Linear flow. Limited response length. No collaborative editing. Content tied to the conversation thread.

Example use: "What are the top five project management methodologies?" or "Draft a short email declining a meeting invitation."

Pages

Best for: Working with AI output collaboratively. Editing and refining Copilot responses. Sharing AI-assisted content with colleagues. Building a document together with AI support.

Limitations: Less formatting control than Word. Not built for very long documents. Collaboration features depend on your organization's Microsoft 365 setup.

Example use: Your team is brainstorming a new product strategy. One person prompts Copilot for a competitive analysis, another asks for a SWOT analysis, a third for customer persona summaries. It all lands in a shared Page where the team can edit, reorganize, and refine.

Notebooks

Best for: Long-form content generation. Detailed prompts that require extended instructions. Creating first drafts of substantial documents.

Limitations: Less collaborative than Pages. Primarily a single-user tool. Output still needs to move to Word, PowerPoint, or another tool for final formatting.

Example use: You need a 3,000-word first draft of a policy document, a comprehensive analysis of a market segment, or a detailed training guide.

A Simple Decision Framework

- Need a quick answer? **Chat.**
- Need to work with AI output and share it? **Pages.**
- Need a long, detailed document? **Notebooks.**
- Need a final, polished, formatted document? Start in **Notebooks**, finish in **Word.**

Collaboration Features in Pages

Collaboration is what distinguishes Pages from every other Copilot surface, so it is worth a closer look.

Sharing and Permissions

Share a Page by clicking the Share button and entering names or email addresses of colleagues in your organization. Permissions are:

- **Can edit:** The person can modify the Page content and use Copilot within it.
- **Can view:** The person can read the Page but cannot make changes.

Shared Pages appear in the recipients' Copilot app, so they can find and access them easily.

Working Together in Real Time

When multiple people edit a Page simultaneously, you see each other's cursors and changes in real time (similar to co-authoring in Word or Google Docs). Each person can also use Copilot independently — you might ask for a budget breakdown while your colleague asks for an executive summary. Both outputs appear in the Page, and either person can edit either section.

This creates a genuinely new workflow: **collaborative AI-assisted writing.** Instead of one person drafting a document and sending it around for edits, the team builds the document together, each person using AI to accelerate their contribution.

Practical Collaboration Scenarios

Meeting follow-ups. After a meeting, share a Page with all attendees. One person asks Copilot to summarize the meeting notes (from a Teams transcript or a shared document). Others add their own notes, action items, and follow-up questions. The Page becomes the living record of the meeting's outcomes.

Project planning. Create a Page for a new project. One team member prompts Copilot for a project charter template. Another asks for a risk assessment. A third generates a timeline. Everyone refines together.

Content creation. A marketing team is creating a blog series. They share a Page where each person owns a different topic. Each person uses Copilot to generate their draft, and the team edits each other's work in the same Page.

Tips for Getting the Most Out of Pages and Notebooks

Start in chat, move to Pages. Do not jump straight to Pages for every task. Start with a quick chat prompt to confirm Copilot understands what you want. Once you get a response heading in the right direction, move it to a Page for refinement.

Use Notebooks for the heavy lifting. If you know you need long-form content, go straight to a Notebook. Write a detailed prompt and let Copilot generate a comprehensive response. Then move the output to a Page (for collaboration) or to Word (for final formatting).

Do not over-collaborate. Pages are great for teams, but too many simultaneous editors create confusion. Two to four collaborators is usually the sweet spot. For larger teams, have one person consolidate input from a shared Page into a final document.

Save important Pages. Pages are easy to lose track of when you create many. Name them clearly and organize by project or topic. The Copilot app shows recent Pages, but a meaningful title helps when you are hunting for something specific.

Iterate on Notebook prompts. The prompt area is large for a reason — use it. A detailed, well-structured prompt produces dramatically better output than a brief one. If your first result is off, revise the prompt rather than trying to fix the output.

Real-World Workflow: Collaborative Research Document

Your team of four needs to produce a competitive analysis report for an upcoming strategy meeting. Here is how to use Pages and Notebooks together.

Step 1: Generate the Framework in a Notebook

One team member opens a Notebook and writes a detailed prompt:

> Create a competitive analysis framework for a B2B SaaS company in the project management space. Include these sections: Market Overview, Competitor Profiles (analyze Asana, Monday.com, Jira, and ClickUp), Feature Comparison Matrix, Pricing Comparison, Strengths and Weaknesses for each competitor, Market Trends, and Strategic Recommendations. For each competitor profile, include company background, target market, key features, recent developments, and market position. Make the analysis approximately 2,500 words.

Copilot generates a comprehensive framework. The team member reviews, makes initial edits, and copies the content.

Step 2: Move to a Shared Page

The team member creates a Page, pastes the content from the Notebook, and shares it with the other three team members with editing permissions.

Step 3: Divide and Conquer

Each team member takes responsibility for a section:

- Person A refines the Market Overview, asking Copilot: "Expand the market overview with current market size and growth projections for the project management SaaS space."
- Person B works on the Competitor Profiles, asking Copilot: "Update the Asana profile with their latest product announcements and pricing changes."
- Person C builds out the Feature Comparison Matrix, asking Copilot: "Create a detailed comparison table of features across all four competitors, including task management, reporting, integrations, and mobile capabilities."
- Person D focuses on Strategic Recommendations, asking Copilot: "Based on the competitor analysis above, generate five strategic recommendations for differentiation."

All four work simultaneously in the same Page, seeing each other's contributions and edits in real time.

Step 4: Review and Refine Together

The team reviews the complete document together. They ask Copilot for a final pass:

> Review this competitive analysis for consistency in tone and depth. Are there any gaps in the analysis that should be addressed?

Copilot flags a few thin areas and suggests additions.

Step 5: Move to Word for Final Formatting

Once the content is solid, one team member copies the Page into a Word document, applies the company's formatting template, adds a cover page and table of contents, and prepares it for distribution.

Total time: about two hours for a comprehensive competitive analysis that typically takes one to two days of individual research and writing.

Key Takeaways

- Pages are collaborative AI canvases — edit, share, and co-author content with Copilot assistance in real time.
- Notebooks are designed for long-form content generation, allowing longer prompts and longer outputs than standard chat.
- Use chat for quick tasks, Pages for collaborative work, and Notebooks for substantial content generation.
- Pages support real-time collaboration where multiple people can edit and use Copilot simultaneously.
- Start in chat or Notebooks, then move to Pages for refinement and collaboration, and to Word for final formatting.
- Name and organize your Pages clearly to keep track of them as you create more.

Chapter 17: Think Deeper — Extended Reasoning

Most of the time, Copilot responds in a few seconds. You ask a question, it generates an answer, the conversation moves forward. For everyday tasks — drafting emails, summarizing documents, answering factual questions — that speed is exactly what you want.

But some questions deserve more than a fast answer. When you are wrestling with a complex decision, analyzing a nuanced problem, or thinking through a multi-step challenge, a quick response can feel shallow. It gives you an answer, not necessarily a well-reasoned one. It may miss edge cases, overlook tradeoffs, or skip considerations a more careful thinker would catch.

Think Deeper is Copilot's answer. It is an extended reasoning mode that takes longer — sometimes 30 seconds, sometimes a full minute or more — and produces responses that are more thorough, more nuanced, and more carefully reasoned. Under the hood, Think Deeper is backed by OpenAI's GPT-5.4 Thinking model (rolled out to Copilot in March 2026), with the newer GPT-5.5 Thinking model now rolling out across Copilot Chat, Word, Excel, and PowerPoint. Both are designed to work through complex problems step by step before generating a final answer; which one you actually hit depends on the surface you are using.

This chapter covers what Think Deeper is, when to use it, what kinds of problems it handles well, and its current limitations. We will close with practical examples showing the difference it makes.

What Think Deeper Actually Does

When you use Think Deeper, Copilot does not just generate a response — it reasons through the problem first. The difference between someone answering off the top of their head and someone sitting down, thinking for a while, and then giving you a considered response.

Technically, Think Deeper uses "reasoning models" (or "thinking models") that spend additional compute time working through the problem internally before producing output. The model creates an internal chain of thought: considers different angles, evaluates potential answers, checks its own reasoning for errors, and produces a final response that reflects the deeper analysis.

You do not see the full internal reasoning (though Copilot sometimes shows a brief "thinking" summary). What you see is the final result — typically longer, more structured, and more carefully argued than a standard response.

Speed vs. Depth

The tradeoff is simple: Think Deeper is slower. A standard Copilot response takes two to five seconds. A Think Deeper response takes 15 to 60 seconds, occasionally longer for particularly complex problems. Not a bug — the point. The model is using that time to think more carefully.

Think Deeper is not appropriate for every question. Ask "What time is it in Tokyo?" or "Write a short thank-you email" and Think Deeper is overkill — you wait longer for no meaningful improvement. Save it for questions where depth actually matters.

How to Activate Think Deeper

In the Copilot interface, a model selector lets you choose between conversation modes. The exact interface varies slightly depending on whether you are using Copilot on the web, in the app, or within Microsoft 365, but the core options are:

Auto: Copilot picks the model based on the complexity of your prompt. Simple questions get a faster model; complex ones may get a reasoning model. The default, and a fine choice most of the time.

Quick Response: Forces a fast model. Quick but may lack depth on complex topics. Good for simple tasks where speed matters.

Think Deeper: Forces Copilot's most capable reasoning model. Slower but more thorough. Use it when you specifically want deeper analysis.

To select Think Deeper, click the model selector (usually near the text input area) and choose it before submitting your prompt. Switch back to Auto or Quick Response at any time.

When to Use Think Deeper

Think Deeper earns its keep in specific situations. The categories where it consistently outperforms standard responses:

Complex Analysis and Decision-Making

When you are weighing options with multiple variables, tradeoffs, and consequences, Think Deeper produces significantly better output.

Example prompt for standard Copilot: > Should our company switch from Slack to Microsoft Teams?

Standard response: A list of pros and cons — maybe five bullets each. Helpful but surface-level.

Same prompt with Think Deeper: A structured analysis that considers your specific situation (if you provide context), weighing factors like cost, user experience, integration with existing tools, migration complexity, training, and organizational change management. It may identify tradeoffs you had not considered and suggest a phased approach with specific evaluation criteria.

Multi-Step Problem Solving

When a question requires working through several logical steps, Think Deeper handles the chain of reasoning more reliably.

> We are launching a product in three markets simultaneously: US, UK, and Japan. Each market has different regulatory requirements, pricing norms, and distribution channels. How should we sequence our go-to-market activities to maximize our chances of success while keeping the launch coordinated?

Think Deeper works through the regulatory, pricing, and logistical considerations for each market, identifies dependencies between the launches, and proposes a sequenced plan that accounts for the complexity.

Nuanced Questions Without Clear Answers

Some questions have no single right answer. They require balancing competing priorities, understanding context, and making judgment calls. Think Deeper handles ambiguity better than standard responses.

> How should a 45-year-old with moderate risk tolerance, a paid-off house, two kids approaching college age, and a desire to retire at 60 think about their investment allocation?

Standard Copilot gives you generic financial advice. Think Deeper weighs the specific constraints — college expenses coming in a few years, a 15-year horizon to retirement, the paid-off house as an asset, moderate risk tolerance — and produces a more personalized, nuanced analysis.

Logic and Reasoning Puzzles

Think Deeper is significantly better at logic problems, math reasoning, and puzzles that require step-by-step deduction.

> A farmer has a fox, a chicken, and a sack of grain. He needs to cross a river in a boat that can only carry him and one item at a time. If left unattended, the fox will eat the chicken, and the chicken will eat the grain. How can the farmer get everything across safely?

Standard Copilot can solve this classic puzzle. Think Deeper handles more complex variations and novel logic problems more reliably.

Writing Complex Documents

For documents that require careful argumentation — legal analyses, policy recommendations, research syntheses, technical evaluations — Think Deeper produces more coherent, better-structured output.

> Write an analysis of the ethical implications of using AI-generated content in journalism, considering perspectives from journalists, publishers, readers, and AI developers. Address the tensions between

efficiency and accuracy, transparency and competitive advantage, and innovation and trust.

Think Deeper produces a more balanced, thorough analysis that grapples with the tensions rather than just listing arguments.

When Not to Use Think Deeper

Think Deeper is the wrong tool for:

Simple factual questions. "What is the capital of France?" gains nothing from extended reasoning. Quick Response or Auto handles these.

Routine writing tasks. Drafting a standard email, generating a meeting agenda, or writing social media captions does not need deeper reasoning. Standard Copilot does these fine.

Speed-critical situations. If you need an answer in the next five seconds, Think Deeper's 30–60 second processing time is a problem. Use Quick Response.

Tasks where the bottleneck is information, not reasoning. If Copilot lacks the data it needs — internal company metrics, personal preferences, domain-specific knowledge — Think Deeper will not magically acquire it. It will reason more carefully about what it does know, but it cannot reason about what it does not.

Very short conversations. Think Deeper works best with substantial context. A one-sentence prompt often does not give the reasoning model enough material to show its advantage over standard responses.

Practical Examples

Concrete examples showing the difference Think Deeper makes.

Example 1: Strategic Planning

Prompt: > I am the owner of a 15-person digital marketing agency. Our revenue has been flat for two years at about $2 million annually. Our three largest clients represent 60% of revenue. We primarily offer SEO, PPC, and social media management. I want to grow to $4 million in the next three years. What is my best path forward?

Standard response: A generic list: diversify services, hire more, market yourself better, raise prices.

Think Deeper response: Identifies client concentration risk as the most urgent issue, breaks down growth into specific revenue targets per year, evaluates three growth strategies (new service lines, new client acquisition, larger engagements with existing clients) with realistic estimates, lays out the hiring and operational implications of each approach, and flags the specific risks of growing too fast (quality dilution, cash flow problems) versus too slowly (continued stagnation).

Example 2: Comparing Technical Approaches

Prompt: > We need to choose between building a custom integration between our CRM and ERP systems or purchasing a middleware solution like MuleSoft or Workato. Our IT team has four developers, we have 12 months, and our budget is $200,000. What should we consider?

Think Deeper response: Evaluates the build-vs.-buy question across dimensions standard responses often miss — total cost of ownership (not just initial cost), ongoing maintenance burden on a four-person team, time to value, flexibility for future integrations, vendor lock-in risks, and the opportunity cost of having developers build middleware instead of core business features. Likely recommends a hybrid approach and explains why.

Example 3: Ethical Dilemma

Prompt: > A manager discovers that an employee has been using AI to complete a significant portion of their work, which the company's policy does not explicitly address. The employee's output quality has improved and they are meeting all deadlines. Should the manager address this, and if so, how?

Think Deeper response: Instead of a simple yes/no, considers multiple angles — transparency and trust, the difference between using AI as a tool and misrepresenting capabilities, the precedent it sets for the team, the company's obligation to create clear policies, the employee's reasonable expectation that useful tools are acceptable, and the practical reality that prohibiting AI use may be unenforceable. Suggests a constructive approach rather than a punitive one and recommends policy actions.

Tips for Better Think Deeper Prompts

Give it context worth reasoning about.

Provide background. The more context you give, the more useful the reasoning. Include relevant constraints, stakeholders, history, and goals.

Ask for analysis, not just answers. "What should I do?" gets a recommendation. "Analyze the tradeoffs and help me think through this decision" gets a more thorough response.

Specify what you care about. "Prioritize cost efficiency" or "I care most about long-term sustainability, not short-term results" focuses the reasoning.

Ask it to consider counterarguments. "What are the strongest arguments against your recommendation?" pushes Think Deeper toward balance.

Request structured output. "Organize your analysis with clear sections for each option, including pros, cons, risks, and your assessment" produces more usable output.

Current Limitations

Think Deeper is powerful but not perfect.

It is still an AI. Extended reasoning does not eliminate the fundamental limitations of large language models. Think Deeper can still hallucinate, make errors, and miss considerations it has no data on.

It does not access real-time information differently. Think Deeper uses the same Bing Search grounding as standard Copilot. It reasons more carefully about the information it finds, but it does not have access to different or better sources.

Usage may be limited. Depending on your plan, you may have a limited number of Think Deeper queries per day. Microsoft adjusts these limits, so check your current plan details.

It can over-reason. Sometimes Think Deeper produces overly complex analysis of a straightforward question. If you find yourself thinking "this is more analysis than I needed," the question was better suited for Auto or Quick Response.

It does not learn between sessions. Think Deeper does not remember previous conversations (unless you are within the same session). Each query is independent.

Key Takeaways

- Think Deeper uses specialized reasoning models that take more time but produce more thorough, nuanced responses.
- Use it for complex analysis, multi-step problem solving, nuanced decisions, and writing that requires careful argumentation.
- Do not use it for simple questions, routine tasks, or situations where speed matters more than depth.
- Provide substantial context in your prompts — Think Deeper works best when it has enough information to reason about.
- Think Deeper is slower by design. The 15–60 seconds of processing time is the model working through the problem step by step.
- It is available through the model selector in the Copilot interface, alongside Auto and Quick Response modes.
- Despite its name, Think Deeper is still an AI tool with the same fundamental limitations as any large language model. It reasons more carefully, but it can still make mistakes.

Chapter 18: Copilot Vision

Every feature we have covered so far works with text. You type words, Copilot reads them, it responds with words (or images, in Designer's case). Copilot Vision breaks that pattern. Instead of reading your text, it looks at your screen.

Copilot Vision lets Copilot see and understand what is displayed in your browser or on your screen. Ask it questions about what you are looking at, get help understanding web pages, and have conversations grounded in visual content rather than typed descriptions.

Vision is generally available as of May 2026 on Windows, macOS, Microsoft Edge, iOS, and Android. It works for users signed in with a personal Microsoft account; users signed in with an Entra ID work account currently cannot access Vision, which is a meaningful limitation if your day-to-day Copilot use is on a corporate identity. Microsoft 365 Personal, Family, and Premium subscribers get extended usage limits. This chapter covers what Vision can do, its current limitations, the privacy considerations to understand, practical use cases, and where the feature is heading.

What Copilot Vision Is

Copilot Vision gives Copilot the ability to see. When enabled, Copilot can analyze the content of web pages you are viewing in Microsoft Edge, or what is displayed on your screen more broadly when you opt in.

Multimodal AI models — models that process both text and images — make this possible. When Vision is active, Copilot takes a visual snapshot of what you are looking at, processes it through these models, and generates responses based on both the text and visual elements on the page.

The difference between describing a painting to someone over the phone and standing next to them in the gallery. When Copilot can see what you see, the conversation becomes faster and more natural.

What Vision Is Not

Copilot Vision is not a screen recording tool. It does not continuously monitor your screen or store images of what you are viewing. When you ask a question, it captures a snapshot of the current view, processes it, and discards the image. It is also not an accessibility tool in the traditional sense — it does not provide screen reader functionality or replace assistive technologies.

Current Capabilities

Vision's capabilities focus on specific scenarios. Here is what it can do today.

Understanding Web Pages

Browsing a website in Microsoft Edge with Vision enabled, you can ask Copilot questions about what you see:

- "What is this page about?" — Copilot reads both the text and the visual layout to provide a summary.
- "What product is being shown here?" — Copilot identifies products, images, and visual content on the page.
- "Can you read the text in this image?" — If a web page has text embedded in images (common in infographics, banners, and social media posts), Copilot extracts and reads it.
- "Compare the two products shown on this page." — On a comparison page, Copilot analyzes the visual layout and provides a structured comparison.

Interpreting Visual Content

Vision is particularly useful for visual content that is hard to describe in text:

- **Charts and graphs:** "What does this chart show? What are the key trends?" Copilot reads bar charts, line graphs, pie charts, and other common visualizations.
- **Screenshots:** Looking at a screenshot of an error message, a settings page, or a software interface, ask "What does this error mean?" or "How do I change this setting?"

- **Maps and diagrams:** Copilot interprets maps, flowcharts, and architectural diagrams, though accuracy varies with complexity.
- **Tables and data:** Complex tables rendered as images (rather than HTML tables) can be read and interpreted.

Helping with Shopping and Research

A practical application many users have found useful: shopping assistance. On a product page, you can ask:

- "Is this a good deal for this type of product?"
- "What are the key specifications of this item?"
- "Can you find similar products at a lower price?"

Copilot reads the product page visually and responds based on what it sees, combined with its general knowledge and Bing search capabilities.

Assisting with Learning

When you are reading educational content — a textbook page, a tutorial, a documentation site — Vision helps you understand the material:

- "Explain this diagram in simple terms."
- "I do not understand the formula shown here. Can you break it down?"
- "What is the main concept being illustrated in this figure?"

How to Enable and Use Copilot Vision

Availability depends on your account type, region, and Microsoft's rollout schedule. The general process:

In Microsoft Edge:

1. Open Microsoft Edge and sign in with your Microsoft account.
2. Open the Copilot sidebar (click the Copilot icon in the toolbar or press the keyboard shortcut).
3. Look for the Vision toggle in the Copilot panel — typically a camera icon, a "Vision" label, or a toggle in Copilot settings.

4. Enable Vision. A notification confirms that Copilot can now see the content of your current browser tab.
5. Navigate to any web page and ask Copilot questions about what you see.

In the Copilot app:

The Copilot desktop and mobile apps support Vision both through native integration on Windows, macOS, iOS, and Android, and through screenshot sharing. Take a screenshot, share it with Copilot, then ask questions about it — more manual than the real-time Edge integration, but works across any application.

What to Expect

Vision is mature enough for everyday use, but a few things are worth knowing:

- Availability can vary across platforms and regions as Microsoft continues to expand the feature.
- Response times may run slightly longer than text-only interactions because the model is processing visual data.
- Accuracy varies. Simple, well-structured pages produce excellent results. Complex, cluttered pages can confuse the model.
- Some website content may not be processed due to technical limitations or content restrictions.

Privacy Considerations

Vision raises real privacy questions. Microsoft has built in several safeguards.

What Copilot Sees

When Vision is active, Copilot can see the content of the browser tab you are viewing:

- Text, images, layouts, and interactive elements on the page.
- Any personal information displayed — your email inbox, your bank account page, your social media profile.
- A snapshot of the current view, not a continuous stream.

What Microsoft Does with the Data

According to Microsoft's privacy documentation for Vision:

- Visual data is processed to generate responses and is not stored long-term.
- For consumer accounts, Microsoft's standard Copilot privacy terms apply.
- For commercial and enterprise accounts, commercial data protections apply — your data is not used to train AI models.

What You Should Do

Even with these protections, use common sense:

Do not enable Vision on sensitive pages. Viewing financial accounts, medical records, or confidential business documents, ask whether you actually need Vision active. For a general question, type it without Vision.

Be aware of what is visible. Vision only sees the active tab. But if that tab contains sensitive information in a sidebar, notification banner, or embedded widget, Copilot processes that content too.

Disable Vision when you do not need it. No benefit to leaving it on. Toggle it off when you are done.

Understand your organization's policies. If you are using Copilot at work, IT may have policies about Vision. Some organizations disable the feature entirely. Check before using it with work-related content.

Practical Use Cases

Scenarios where Vision adds genuine value.

Technical Troubleshooting

You are setting up a new piece of software and hit a configuration screen with a dozen settings you do not understand. Instead of describing the screen in text, enable Vision and ask:

> What do each of these settings do? Which ones should I change for a standard home network setup?

Copilot reads the labels, input fields, and any on-screen help text, then explains each setting and recommends values for your described use case.

Data Interpretation

You are viewing a dashboard with several charts and graphs — an analytics tool, a financial report, a BI dashboard. Ask:

> What are the three most important insights from this dashboard?

Copilot analyzes the charts, identifies trends, and highlights the most significant data points. Faster than describing each chart in text and asking for interpretation.

Accessibility and Comprehension

You are reading an academic paper or technical documentation with complex diagrams, formulas, or illustrations. Ask:

> Explain this diagram to me like I am a beginner in this field.

Copilot interprets the visual content and provides a simplified explanation. Particularly useful for visual learners or anyone encountering a new domain for the first time.

Shopping Decisions

You are comparison shopping and have a product page open with specifications, reviews, and pricing. You ask:

> Is this laptop a good choice for someone who needs to run video editing software and has a budget of $1,500?

Copilot reads the specs from the page, evaluates them against your stated needs, and provides a recommendation — without you manually extracting and typing the specs.

Learning from Videos and Tutorials

Paused on a frame of an instructional video or looking at a step in a tutorial, you can ask:

> I am on step 4 of this tutorial. What am I supposed to do next? I do not understand the diagram.

Copilot interprets the visual instructions and provides a clear explanation.

Current Limitations

Vision is impressive, but it has clear limitations.

Edge gets the deepest browser integration. Vision works most seamlessly inside Microsoft Edge for live browser content. On Chrome, Firefox, or Safari, the workaround is taking screenshots and sharing them with Copilot — less seamless but functional. Native Vision support on Windows, macOS, iOS, and Android covers screen and app content beyond the browser.

Complex visuals can be misinterpreted. Dense infographics, overlapping UI elements, or poorly designed pages can confuse the model. If a page is hard for a human to parse, it will be hard for Copilot too.

It cannot interact with pages. Vision sees what is on the page but cannot click buttons, fill forms, or navigate for you. An observer, not an actor. (Agentic capabilities that take actions on your behalf are a separate, earlier-stage development track.)

Dynamic content gets missed. Animations, videos, or content that changes as you scroll — Copilot sees only a static snapshot of the current view. Moving content or content below the fold is not captured.

Accuracy varies. Vision is less reliable than text-only interactions. Expect it to be right most of the time for simple pages and less consistently accurate for complex ones. Always verify important details.

Entra ID work accounts cannot use Vision. This is a hard limitation for the workplace audience this book serves. If you sign in to Copilot with a corporate identity, Vision is not available; you have to switch to a personal Microsoft account to use it.

What to Expect Going Forward

Copilot Vision represents an important direction for AI assistants. The ability to see and understand visual content makes AI more useful in situations where text alone falls short.

Based on Microsoft's public roadmap and the trajectory of multimodal AI:

Broader platform and identity support. Vision currently delivers its deepest browser integration in Microsoft Edge and is limited to personal Microsoft accounts. Expect Microsoft to extend coverage across more browsers, deepen integration into the Copilot app, and eventually open the feature to commercial Entra ID accounts as data-handling assurances catch up.

Improved accuracy. As multimodal models improve, Vision's ability to interpret complex visuals will get better. Charts, diagrams, and dense layouts that confuse it today will be handled more reliably.

Deeper integration with Microsoft 365. Vision-like capabilities may eventually extend to Word, Excel, PowerPoint, and other Microsoft 365 apps — helping you work with visual content inside your documents, not just on web pages.

Agentic capabilities. The long-term vision (no pun intended) is for AI assistants to not just see your screen but to take actions on your behalf — clicking buttons, filling forms, navigating between apps. A separate development track that builds on the same multimodal foundation.

Vision is a useful tool with real but evolving capabilities. Experiment with it, understand its privacy implications, and feed your experience back to Microsoft through the built-in feedback mechanisms. User feedback continues to shape how the feature develops.

Key Takeaways

- Copilot Vision lets Copilot see and understand your screen, enabling questions and conversations about visual content.
- It works on Windows, macOS, Edge, iOS, and Android for personal Microsoft accounts; commercial Entra ID accounts currently cannot access it.
- Vision excels at interpreting web pages, charts, product pages, error messages, and visual tutorials.
- Privacy matters — be thoughtful about enabling Vision on pages with sensitive information, and disable it when not needed.
- The feature cannot interact with pages, only observe them. It sees static snapshots, not dynamic content.
- Expect Vision to improve significantly as multimodal AI technology matures and as Microsoft expands coverage across browsers, applications, and identity types.

Part V: Prompting and Technique

"The science of today is the technology of tomorrow."

— Edward Teller

Chapter 19: Prompting Fundamentals

If one skill separates people who find Copilot merely interesting from people who find it indispensable, it is prompting. Not because prompting is a technical discipline reserved for programmers — it is not. Because most people never pause to think about how they phrase requests to an AI, and a handful of deliberate adjustments transform vague, generic answers into precise, useful ones.

This chapter teaches those adjustments. You will learn what makes a prompt effective in Microsoft Copilot specifically, how to structure your requests so the AI understands exactly what you want, and how to avoid the common mistakes that lead to disappointing results. By the end, you will have twenty ready-to-use prompt templates.

What Makes a Good Prompt for Copilot

A good prompt is not about memorizing special phrases or insider tricks. It is about clarity. Copilot is powered by large language models that are remarkably capable at interpreting natural language, but they cannot read your mind. The more precisely you communicate what you want, the better the result.

Think of it this way: if you walked up to a brilliant but brand-new colleague and said "help me with the thing," they would need a dozen follow-up questions before they could be useful. Copilot is in the same position, except it usually will not ask. Instead, it makes assumptions — and those assumptions may or may not match what you had in mind.

A good Copilot prompt has five qualities:

1. **It is specific.** Instead of "write something about marketing," you say "write a 500-word blog post about email marketing strategies for small e-commerce businesses."
2. **It provides context.** Copilot does not know your situation unless you tell it. Who is the audience? What is the goal? What constraints exist?
3. **It defines the format.** Do you want a list? A paragraph? A table? A formal report? Say so.

4. **It sets constraints.** Word count, tone, topics to avoid, level of detail — these boundaries focus the output.
5. **It assigns a role when helpful.** Telling Copilot to respond as a specific type of expert shapes its vocabulary, depth, and approach.

You do not need all five in every prompt. A quick factual question — "What is the population of Portugal?" — needs no role or format. But the more complex your request, the more these elements matter.

The Five Elements of an Effective Prompt

Break down the anatomy of a strong prompt. These five elements are a toolkit you draw from whenever you need better results.

1. Role

The role tells Copilot what perspective to adopt. It shapes vocabulary, depth, and approach.

> You are an experienced marketing consultant who specializes in helping small businesses grow their email lists.

Compare the response you get from that setup versus simply asking "tell me about email marketing." The role creates focus and expertise.

2. Task

The task is the core of your prompt — what you want Copilot to do. Be direct. Use action verbs: write, analyze, compare, summarize, explain, create, list, evaluate, draft, outline.

> Write a comparison of three email marketing platforms suitable for a business with fewer than 1,000 subscribers.

3. Context

Context is the background Copilot needs to do the task well — your industry, audience, experience level, timeline, or any relevant constraints.

> My business is a handmade jewelry shop on Etsy. I have about 400 email subscribers and a monthly marketing budget of $50. I currently send emails manually through Gmail.

4. Format

Tell Copilot how to structure the output. Eliminates guesswork and gives you results you can use immediately.

> Present this as a table with columns for platform name, monthly price, key features, ease of use rating, and a one-sentence summary.

5. Constraints

Constraints are the guardrails. They tell Copilot what to include, what to exclude, and what boundaries to respect.

> Keep the comparison under 600 words. Only include platforms with Free tiers. Write in a casual, friendly tone. Do not recommend Mailchimp, as I have already tried it.

Putting It All Together

A complete prompt combining all five elements:

> You are a marketing consultant who specializes in helping small e-commerce businesses. Compare three email marketing platforms suitable for a handmade jewelry shop on Etsy with about 400 subscribers and a $50 monthly marketing budget. I currently send emails manually through Gmail. Present this as a table with columns for platform name, monthly price, key features, ease of use, and a one-sentence summary, followed by a brief recommendation. Keep it under 600 words, only include platforms with Free tiers, do not recommend Mailchimp, and write in a casual, friendly tone.

That prompt gets you a genuinely useful answer on the first try. Thirty seconds to write, five minutes of back-and-forth saved.

Specific vs. Vague: The Difference That Matters Most

The single biggest improvement most people can make is being more specific. Before-and-after:

Vague: "Help me with my resume." **Specific:** "Review my resume for a senior marketing manager position at a tech company. Focus on whether my bullet points use strong action verbs and quantifiable achievements. Here is my resume: [paste resume]."

Vague: "Write an email." **Specific:** "Write a professional email to my manager requesting two days of remote work per week. My reasons are a long commute (90 minutes each way) and higher productivity at home. Keep it under 200 words and maintain a respectful, collaborative tone."

Vague: "Explain Excel formulas." **Specific:** "Explain the VLOOKUP function in Excel to someone who has never used it. Use an analogy to make it intuitive. Show one simple example with sample data. Keep it to three paragraphs."

Vague: "Give me presentation ideas." **Specific:** "Suggest five creative presentation topics for a 15-minute talk at a nonprofit board meeting about increasing volunteer retention. The audience is board members aged 40–65 who are not tech-savvy."

The specific versions give Copilot a clear target. You are not limiting creativity — you are focusing it.

Common Beginner Mistakes

Certain patterns consistently lead to disappointing results.

Mistake 1: Being Too Brief

One-sentence prompts almost always produce generic responses. Copilot is not a search engine — it does not just need a query. It needs instructions. Do not be afraid to write a full paragraph or more. The small investment pays off in much better output.

Mistake 2: Asking Multiple Unrelated Questions at Once

"What is the capital of France, how do I fix a leaky faucet, and can you write me a poem about dogs?" Copilot attempts all three, and the quality of each suffers. Focus on one task at a time, or at least number your questions clearly so Copilot can address each separately.

Mistake 3: Not Providing Examples

If you want output in a specific style or format, show Copilot an example. "Write product descriptions like this one: [example]" beats describing the style in abstract terms.

Mistake 4: Forgetting to Specify the Audience

A financial analysis for a CFO looks very different from one for a college student. Always tell Copilot who will be reading the output.

Mistake 5: Assuming Copilot Remembers Previous Conversations

Each new conversation starts fresh. Copilot does not retain information from past chats unless you are working within a persistent context like Microsoft 365 Copilot, where it can access organizational data. If context from a previous conversation matters, paste it in or summarize it.

Mistake 6: Not Iterating

Your first prompt does not have to be perfect. Treat it as a starting point. If the response is close but not quite right, tell Copilot what to adjust. "This is good, but make the tone more formal and add a section about pricing" is a perfectly valid follow-up. The best results often come from two or three rounds of refinement.

Mistake 7: Overcomplicating the Prompt

There is a balance between specificity and overload. Unnecessary jargon, contradictory instructions, or walls of tangential detail muddy the waters. Write naturally. Pretend you are giving instructions to a smart coworker who is new to the project.

Copilot-Specific Prompting Tips

Copilot has some unique characteristics that affect how you should prompt compared to other AI assistants.

Copilot Uses Bing Search Grounding

Unlike some AI assistants that work purely from training data, Copilot can search the web in real time through Bing. You can ask about current events, recent news, today's weather, or live information and expect reasonably up-to-date answers with citations.

When you want Copilot to use the web, phrase your prompt accordingly: "Search for the latest reviews of the iPhone 17 and summarize the pros and cons from three different sources." If you want an answer purely from Copilot's knowledge without a search, say so — though Copilot may search anyway depending on the mode.

Modes Change How Copilot Responds

Copilot offers different modes — Quick Response, Auto, and Think Deeper — that affect depth and quality. For a simple factual question, Quick Response is fine. For a complex problem, Think Deeper gives the model more room to reason.

Match your prompting to the mode. In Think Deeper, you can present a more complex, multi-part problem. In Quick Response, keep prompts focused and straightforward.

Microsoft 365 Integration Changes the Game

When you are using Copilot within Microsoft 365 — Word, Excel, PowerPoint, Outlook, Teams — you do not always need to provide context manually. Copilot can reference your documents, emails, meeting transcripts, and files.

In Word, prompt: "Summarize this document in three bullet points." In Outlook: "Draft a reply agreeing to the meeting time and suggesting we add the marketing team." In Teams: "What decisions were made in today's standup meeting?"

The fundamentals still apply, but the context element is often handled by the app itself.

Copilot Responds Well to Natural Language

You do not need special syntax, programming-style commands, or technical formatting to get good results. Write the way you would speak to a colleague. Copilot's models are trained to understand conversational English exceptionally well.

That said, if you are pasting in large blocks of text, separate your instructions from the source material clearly. Put your instructions first, then add a line like "Here is the text to work with:" followed by the pasted content.

20 Prompt Templates for Everyday Use

Twenty templates you can copy, customize, and use immediately. Each uses [brackets] to mark parts you fill in with your own details.

1. Professional Email

```
Write a professional email to [recipient/role] about [topic]. Context: [brief background]. Tone: [polite/formal/friendly]. Keep it under [number] words.
```

2. Meeting Agenda

```
Create a meeting agenda for a [duration]-minute [type of meeting] about [topic]. Attendees: [roles/names]. Include time allocations for each item and end with action items.
```

3. Document Summary

```
Summarize the following [document type] in [number] bullet points. Focus on [key themes/decisions/action items]. Audience: [who will read the summary].

[Paste document text]
```

4. Research Overview

```
Research [topic] and provide a balanced overview. Include: current state, key debates or perspectives, recent developments, and practical implications for [audience/context]. Cite your sources.
```

5. Comparison

```
Compare [option A], [option B], and [option C] for [use case]. Present as a table with columns for [criteria 1], [criteria 2], [criteria 3], and a recommendation. Keep it under [word count] words.
```

6. Explain a Concept

```
Explain [concept] to someone who is [audience description, e.g., "a complete beginner" or "a 12-year-old"]. Use [number] everyday analogies. Keep it to [number] paragraphs.
```

7. Rewrite for Tone

```
Rewrite the following text in a [formal/casual/persuasive/empathetic] tone. Keep the core message the same but adjust the language for [audience].

[Paste text]
```

8. Brainstorming

```
Generate [number] creative ideas for [goal/project]. Context: [relevant details about the situation]. For each idea, include a one-sentence description and one potential challenge.
```

9. Action Plan

```
Create a step-by-step action plan for [goal]. Timeline: [timeframe]. Resources available: [list]. Include milestones, deadlines, and who is responsible for each step.
```

10. Pros and Cons Analysis

```
List the pros and cons of [decision/option]. Context: [your situation]. Consider [specific factors]. Present as two columns. End with a one-paragraph recommendation.
```

11. Social Media Post

```
Write a [platform] post about [topic]. Goal: [inform/engage/promote]. Tone: [professional/casual/inspiring]. Include a strong hook in the first line. Maximum [word/character] count.
```

12. Job Description

Write a job description for a [title] position at [company type]. Key responsibilities: [list]. Required qualifications: [list]. Tone: [professional/startup-casual/formal]. Include information about [benefits/culture/growth opportunities].

13. Feedback Draft

Help me write constructive feedback for [person/role] about [topic]. What went well: [positives]. What needs improvement: [areas]. Tone: [supportive/direct/encouraging]. Keep it professional and specific.

14. Presentation Outline

Create an outline for a [duration]-minute presentation about [topic]. Audience: [description]. Goal: [inform/persuade/train]. Include [number] main sections, key talking points for each, and suggestions for visuals.

15. Data Interpretation

I have the following data: [describe or paste data]. Help me identify [number] key trends or insights. Explain each insight in plain language and suggest one action to take based on it.

16. Customer Response

Write a response to a customer who [describe the situation – complaint, question, request]. Our policy is [relevant policy]. Tone: empathetic and helpful. Offer [specific resolution]. Keep it under [number] sentences.

17. Study Guide

Create a study guide for [subject/exam]. Cover these topics: [list]. For each topic, include: a brief explanation, one example, and one practice question with the answer. Difficulty level: [beginner/intermediate/advanced].

18. Weekly Report

Draft a weekly report for [audience]. Accomplishments this week: [list]. Challenges: [list]. Next week's priorities: [list]. Tone: professional and concise. Format as bullet points with brief context for each item.

19. Decision Framework

```
Help me decide between [option A] and [option B]. My priorities are: [list priorities in order]. My constraints are: [list constraints]. Walk me through the decision systematically and give a recommendation.
```

20. Event Planning Checklist

```
Create a detailed checklist for planning a [type of event] for [number] people. Date: [timeframe]. Budget: [amount]. Include categories for [venue, catering, invitations, etc.] with specific tasks and deadlines.
```

Building the Prompting Habit

Prompting is a skill, and like any skill, it improves with practice. You do not need to memorize frameworks or templates. What you need is the habit of pausing ten seconds before typing and asking yourself three questions:

1. **What exactly do I want?** Not roughly, not vaguely — what specifically would the ideal output look like?
2. **What does Copilot need to know?** What context, constraints, or preferences would help it deliver that ideal output?
3. **How should the output be formatted?** Would a table, a list, or a narrative paragraph serve you best?

Those ten seconds of thinking save you minutes of back-and-forth and deliver dramatically better results. Over time, it becomes automatic. You will find yourself writing clear, effective prompts without thinking about it — and wondering how you ever got by with "help me with the thing."

The next chapter builds on these fundamentals with something more ambitious: how to use Copilot for long, complex tasks that require multiple steps and sustained reasoning.

For a comprehensive library of 78 prompt templates organized by category, see Appendix B.

Chapter 20: Working with Long and Complex Tasks

Most people discover Copilot through quick, single-turn interactions. You ask a question, get an answer, move on. A perfectly valid way to use it — but it barely scratches the surface.

The real power emerges when you use Copilot for tasks too complex, too multi-layered, or too lengthy for a single prompt. Writing a business plan. Analyzing a dataset and drawing conclusions. Drafting a ten-page report. Preparing for a negotiation. These are the tasks where Copilot saves you hours — but only if you know how to manage the process.

This chapter covers how to break big tasks into manageable steps, chain prompts for cumulative results, manage context across a long conversation, and know when to start fresh versus keep building.

Why Single Prompts Fall Short for Complex Work

A single prompt works beautifully for focused tasks: summarize this email, write a thank-you note, explain a concept, generate a table. But when you try to cram an entire complex project into one prompt, problems emerge.

Output gets shallow. Ask Copilot to "write a business plan for a coffee shop" and it produces something covering all the sections — executive summary, market analysis, financial projections — but each section is thin. There is only so much depth a single response can provide.

Important details get missed. Complex tasks have nuances. A business plan needs to account for your specific location, target market, competitive advantages, funding situation. A single prompt cannot convey all of this, and Copilot cannot ask about what you have not mentioned.

You lose control over quality. When everything is generated at once, you cannot course-correct. If the market analysis is based on the wrong assumptions, everything that follows — financial projections, marketing strategy — inherits the error.

The solution is not longer prompts. It is to work in stages.

Breaking Big Tasks into Steps

The most important technique for complex work is decomposition — breaking a big task into a sequence of smaller, manageable steps. This mirrors how you would approach the task yourself and gives you control at every stage.

The Decomposition Process

Start by asking yourself: if I were doing this without AI, what would my steps be? Then use Copilot for each step.

Say you need to write a quarterly business review presentation. Break it down:

1. **Outline the structure.** Ask Copilot to suggest a structure for a quarterly review, specifying your audience and key topics.
2. **Draft each section.** Work through the presentation section by section, providing relevant data and context for each.
3. **Generate insights.** Ask Copilot to identify trends or notable findings from the data you provide.
4. **Refine the narrative.** Once all sections exist, ask Copilot to ensure the overall story is coherent and compelling.
5. **Polish the language.** Final pass for tone, clarity, and consistency.

Each step is a focused interaction where you review, adjust, and approve before moving on. Compare this to a single prompt like "create a quarterly business review presentation" — the staged approach produces dramatically better results.

When You Do Not Know the Steps

Sometimes you are tackling something you have never done before and do not know how to break it down. A perfect first prompt for Copilot:

> I need to [describe the task]. I have never done this before. What are the key steps involved? Break it down into a logical sequence I can work through one step at a time.

Copilot gives you a roadmap, and you work through it step by step — using Copilot as your guide at each stage.

Chaining Prompts

Prompt chaining uses the output from one prompt as input or context for the next. Each prompt builds on what came before, producing a cumulative result no single prompt could achieve.

Sequential Chaining

The simplest form: complete one step, review the result, use it as the foundation for the next.

Step 1: > I am writing a proposal to my manager about implementing a four-day work week at our company. Start by listing the five strongest arguments in favor of a four-day work week, with evidence or statistics for each.

Step 2: > Good. Now list the three strongest counterarguments a skeptical manager might raise, and for each one, write a brief rebuttal.

Step 3: > Now draft the full proposal as a two-page memo. Use the arguments and rebuttals we just developed. Tone: professional and data-driven. Address it to [manager's name] and include a suggested pilot program.

Step 4: > Review this memo for any logical weaknesses or gaps. What might my manager push back on that I have not addressed?

Each step builds on the previous work. By Step 3, Copilot has a rich foundation of arguments, counterarguments, and rebuttals to draw from. The resulting memo is far stronger than if you had asked for it in a single prompt.

Branching Chains

Sometimes you need to explore multiple directions before converging on a final result. That is a branching chain.

> Give me three different angles I could take for a presentation about our company's sustainability efforts. For each angle, give a one-sentence pitch and the type of audience it would work best for.

After reviewing the three angles, you choose the most promising one and dive deeper:

> I like the second angle — focusing on the financial returns of our green initiatives. Develop a detailed outline for a 20-minute presentation using this angle. Audience: the board of directors.

Refinement Chains

Refinement chaining takes a draft and improves it through successive rounds of focused feedback.

Round 1: Generate the initial draft. **Round 2:** "Make the introduction more compelling. Start with a surprising statistic." **Round 3:** "The third section is too long. Cut it to half the length while keeping the key points." **Round 4:** "Add a stronger call to action at the end."

Each round targets a specific aspect of quality. The result is a polished piece that has gone through multiple rounds of focused improvement.

Multi-Turn Strategies

A multi-turn conversation is any interaction that lasts more than one exchange. Most complex tasks will be multi-turn. Strategies for making them productive:

Set the Stage Early

Your first message in a complex, multi-turn conversation should establish the overall goal, your role, and any constraints that apply to the entire task — not just step one.

> I am preparing for a job interview at [company] for a [position]. Over the next several messages, I am going to ask you to help me with different aspects of my preparation. The interview is next Tuesday. I have five years of experience in [field] and my biggest strengths are [list]. Let us start with: what are the most likely interview questions for this role?

This gives Copilot context it can carry throughout the conversation.

Use Explicit Transitions

When you shift from one phase to another, tell Copilot clearly:

> Great, we are done with the interview questions. Now let us move on to a different part of my preparation: reviewing my resume for this specific role.

This prevents Copilot from blending the contexts of different phases.

Summarize and Confirm

For long conversations, periodically summarize what has been accomplished and confirm Copilot is tracking correctly:

> Let me summarize what we have so far: we have the market analysis showing three key trends, a competitive landscape section covering five competitors, and a draft value proposition. Is that consistent with what you have in the conversation? Now let us work on the financial projections section.

Provide Feedback, Not Just Approval

"Looks good" is the least useful thing you can say. If something is good, say what is good about it. If something needs to change, be specific:

- "The tone in the second paragraph is too casual for this audience. Make it more professional."
- "These numbers do not match the data I provided. Recalculate using the figures in my first message."
- "I like the structure but the examples are too generic. Use examples from the healthcare industry."

Specific feedback produces specific improvements.

Managing Context

Every AI conversation has a context window — the total amount of text (your messages and Copilot's responses) the model can "see" at once. In very long conversations, the earliest messages may fall outside what Copilot can actively reference.

Signs of Context Loss

You may notice context loss when:

- Copilot contradicts something it said earlier
- It "forgets" constraints you set at the beginning
- It asks for information you already provided
- The overall coherence of a long project starts to drift

Strategies for Managing Context

Repeat key constraints. If you set important constraints early, restate them when they become relevant again. "Remember, this should be written for a non-technical audience" costs you a few seconds and prevents drift.

Use summary messages. Every five to ten exchanges, summarize the current state of the project. Refreshes Copilot's awareness of the full picture.

Keep one conversation per project. Do not mix unrelated tasks in the same conversation. Each topic deserves its own thread.

Front-load critical information. Put the most important context at the beginning of your prompt, not buried at the end. AI models consistently pay more attention to the start and end of prompts than to the middle.

When to Start Fresh vs. Continue

One of the most practical judgment calls you will make: keep building in the current conversation, or start a new one?

Keep Going When:

- The conversation is still coherent and Copilot is referencing earlier context correctly
- You are iterating on a single deliverable (refining a draft, say)
- The task is a natural continuation of what came before
- You have not exceeded roughly 15–20 exchanges

Start Fresh When:

- Copilot seems to have lost track of earlier context
- You are moving to a fundamentally different task
- The conversation has become cluttered with abandoned directions or corrections

- You want a fresh perspective (sometimes starting over yields better results than trying to redirect a long conversation)
- Response quality has noticeably declined

Starting fresh does not mean losing everything. Copy the best outputs from the previous conversation and paste them into the new one as context: "Here is the outline we developed in a previous session. Now I want to draft Section 3."

Using Think Deeper for Complex Reasoning

Copilot's Think Deeper mode (extended reasoning) is built for tasks that require sustained, multi-step reasoning. It gives the model more time to work through problems before responding and excels where Quick Response or Auto would give you a superficial answer.

When to Use Think Deeper

- Analyzing a complex document and identifying subtle patterns or inconsistencies
- Working through a multi-step math or logic problem
- Comparing multiple options with numerous trade-offs
- Developing a detailed strategy or plan
- Reviewing a contract or policy for potential issues
- Any task where you would say "I need you to really think about this"

Prompting for Think Deeper

In Think Deeper, you can present more complexity in a single prompt. Instead of breaking a problem into tiny steps, present the full problem and let the model reason through it:

> I am deciding whether to lease or buy a car. Here are my specifics: I drive approximately 15,000 miles per year, I plan to keep the car for 5 years, my credit score is 740, I have $5,000 for a down payment, and I live in a state with 6% sales tax. The car I am considering has an MSRP of $35,000. Walk me through the financial analysis of leasing versus buying, including total cost of ownership, monthly payments, and the break-even point. Consider depreciation, interest rates, insurance differences, and any tax implications.

In Think Deeper, Copilot works through all these factors systematically rather than giving you a surface-level comparison.

Combining Think Deeper with Chaining

For the most ambitious tasks, combine Think Deeper with prompt chaining. Use Think Deeper for the steps that require deep analysis, and switch to regular mode for simpler steps like formatting or summarizing.

Practical Example: Building a Complete Project

A complete example using these techniques together for a real-world task: preparing a budget proposal for your department.

Prompt 1 (Decomposition): > I need to prepare a budget proposal for my IT department for next fiscal year. Help me break this into steps. What sections should the proposal include and what information do I need to gather for each?

Prompt 2 (Context and Data): > Here is last year's budget breakdown: [paste data]. And here are the three new initiatives we want to fund: [list]. Help me analyze last year's spending and identify areas where we were over or under budget.

Prompt 3 (Analysis — use Think Deeper): > Based on this analysis, project next year's budget. Account for 4% inflation, the three new initiatives, and the fact that we are adding two new team members. Show your reasoning for each line item.

Prompt 4 (Narrative): > Now draft the executive summary for this proposal. It should be persuasive, concise, and highlight the ROI of the three new initiatives. Audience: the CFO, who is known for being skeptical of IT spending.

Prompt 5 (Review): > Review the full proposal for any gaps, inconsistencies, or weak arguments. What questions might the CFO ask, and how should I prepare to answer them?

Five prompts. Each focused. Each building on the last. The result is a thorough, well-reasoned budget proposal that would have taken you hours from scratch.

Key Takeaways

Working with Copilot on complex tasks is less about any single technique and more about mindset: think of Copilot as a collaborator you are guiding through a process, not a magic box you dump everything into at once.

Break big tasks into steps. Chain your prompts so each one builds on the last. Manage context by summarizing and restating key information. Use Think Deeper when the reasoning demands it. Know when to start fresh.

Master these, and there is almost no task too complex for you and Copilot to tackle together.

Chapter 21: Output Formatting and Control

A common frustration with AI assistants is getting responses in the wrong format. You wanted a concise list and got a five-paragraph essay. You wanted a table and got bullet points. You wanted something you could paste directly into a report and got something that needs twenty minutes of reformatting.

This chapter is about eliminating that frustration. You will learn how to tell Copilot exactly how to structure its output — tables, lists, specific lengths, particular styles — so what you get back is usable without extensive editing. The techniques are simple, but they save an enormous amount of time.

Why Format Matters

Format is not aesthetics. It is usability. A well-formatted response drops straight into an email, a report, a presentation, or a spreadsheet. A poorly formatted response — even with excellent content — creates extra work.

Consider two versions of the same information:

Version A (unformatted): "The three main competitors in the market are Acme Corp, which was founded in 2018 and has revenue of approximately $50 million with 200 employees, and then there is Beta Solutions, founded in 2015, which has revenue of about $120 million and 800 employees, and finally Gamma Tech, which started in 2020 and has revenue of $30 million with 100 employees."

Version B (formatted as a table):

Company	Founded	Revenue	Employees
Acme Corp	2018	$50M	200
Beta Solutions	2015	$120M	800
Gamma Tech	2020	$30M	100

Same information. Version B takes two seconds to read and pastes directly into a slide or spreadsheet.

Tables

Tables are one of the most useful output formats, and Copilot handles them well. The key is telling Copilot you want a table and specifying the columns.

Basic Table Request

```
Compare the three Microsoft 365 plans for businesses. Present as a table with co
lumns for plan name, monthly price per user, storage, and key features.
```

Detailed Table Specifications

When precision matters, be explicit about every aspect:

```
Create a table comparing five programming languages for beginners. Columns: Lang
uage, Difficulty Level (rate 1-5), Best Use Cases, Free Learning Resources, Job
Market Demand (High/Medium/Low). Sort by difficulty level, easiest first.
```

Tables with Analysis

You can ask for a table followed by interpretation:

```
Present the following data as a table, then write a one-paragraph analysis of th
e key trends:

Q1 Sales: $120K, Q2 Sales: $145K, Q3 Sales: $98K, Q4 Sales: $210K
Q1 Returns: 3%, Q2 Returns: 2%, Q3 Returns: 5%, Q4 Returns: 1%
```

Limitations of Tables in Copilot

Tables in Copilot are rendered in Markdown. They look clean in the chat interface but may need minor adjustments when pasted into Word or other applications. If you are using Copilot inside Word, it formats tables using Word's native table features — seamless.

Lists and Bullet Points

Lists are the workhorse format. They are scannable, organized, and easy to work with.

Simple Lists

```
List ten team-building activities suitable for a remote team of 15 people. Budge
t: under $50 per person.
```

Numbered Lists for Sequential Steps

When order matters, ask for numbered lists:

```
Give me a numbered, step-by-step guide to setting up a LinkedIn company page. In
clude what to have prepared before you start.
```

Nested Lists for Hierarchical Information

For complex topics with subtopics:

```
Outline the key areas of project management. Use a nested list format: main cate
gories as top-level items, with 3-4 subtopics under each.
```

Annotated Lists

When you want more than just items:

```
List the top 8 productivity apps for professionals. For each, include: the app n
ame, what it does in one sentence, the price, and one specific use case.
```

Controlling Length

Length control is one of the simplest and highest-impact formatting instructions you can give. Without it, Copilot uses its own judgment about response length — and that judgment may not match your needs.

Word Count Targets

You can specify approximate word counts:

```
Write a 300-word summary of the benefits of remote work.
```

Copilot gets close to the target, typically within 10–20% either direction. If exact length matters, specify a range: "between 250 and 300 words."

Paragraph Limits

For less precise length control:

```
Explain blockchain technology in exactly three paragraphs. First paragraph: what
 it is. Second: how it works. Third: why it matters.
```

Sentence-Level Control

For very concise output:

```
Summarize this article in three sentences. Each sentence should cover a differen
t key point.
```

Character Limits

Useful for social media and other constrained formats:

```
Write a LinkedIn post about our new product launch. Maximum 300 characters inclu
ding spaces.
```

The "Keep It Short" Problem

"Keep it short" often fails because "short" is subjective. Be specific: "Keep it under 200 words," "No more than five bullet points," or "Limit to one paragraph" gives Copilot a clear target.

Tone and Style Control

The words Copilot picks and how it arranges them shift dramatically with your tone instructions.

Common Tone Keywords

Here are tone descriptors that Copilot interprets consistently:

- **Formal:** Corporate, professional, suitable for official communications
- **Casual:** Conversational, relaxed, like talking to a friend
- **Academic:** Scholarly, precise, citation-ready
- **Persuasive:** Compelling, emphasizing benefits and urgency
- **Empathetic:** Warm, understanding, acknowledging emotions
- **Direct:** No filler, no hedging, straight to the point
- **Enthusiastic:** Upbeat, energetic, positive
- **Neutral:** Balanced, objective, no emotional coloring

Combining Tone Descriptors

You can combine descriptors for nuance:

```
Write this in a tone that is professional but warm – like a manager who genuinel
y cares about their team.
```

Matching a Specific Voice

If you have an existing piece of writing whose style you want to replicate:

```
Here is an example of the writing style I want you to match:

[paste example]

Now write a new piece about [topic] using the same style, tone, and sentence str
ucture.
```

This is one of the most powerful formatting techniques available. Copilot is good at analyzing and replicating writing styles.

Structured Output Patterns

Beyond tables and lists, several structured patterns work exceptionally well with Copilot.

SWOT Analysis

```
Perform a SWOT analysis for [company/product/idea]. Present as four clearly labe
led sections: Strengths, Weaknesses, Opportunities, and Threats. Include 3-5 bul
let points in each section.
```

Pros and Cons

```
Give me the pros and cons of [decision]. Format as two columns. End with a one-p
aragraph recommendation based on the balance of evidence.
```

FAQ Format

```
Create an FAQ document for [topic/product/process]. Include 10 questions a [audi
ence type] would likely ask, with concise answers of 2-3 sentences each.
```

Executive Briefing

```
Write an executive briefing on [topic]. Structure: one-paragraph summary, three key findings as bullet points, two recommendations, and one risk to monitor. Total length: under 400 words.
```

Decision Matrix

```
Help me decide between [options]. Create a decision matrix with these criteria: [list criteria]. Rate each option on a scale of 1-5 for each criterion. Calculate total scores and recommend the winner.
```

Formatting for Specific Destinations

Where your Copilot output is going affects how you should request formatting.

For Email

```
Draft an email. Keep paragraphs short (2-3 sentences max). Use a clear subject line. No bullet points in the greeting or sign-off. Professional but not stiff.
```

For Presentations (PowerPoint)

```
Create content for a slide deck. Format each slide as:
- Slide title
- 3-4 bullet points (under 10 words each)
- One speaker note paragraph (what I should say, not what is on the slide)
```

For Reports (Word)

```
Write this as a formal report section with a heading, an introductory paragraph, subheadings for each main point, and a concluding paragraph. Use a professional, third-person tone.
```

For Spreadsheets (Excel)

```
Present this data in a format I can paste into a spreadsheet. Use tab-separated values with a header row. Include columns for [list columns].
```

For Social Media

```
Write three versions of this announcement: one for LinkedIn (professional, 150 words), one for X (casual, under 280 characters), and one for an internal Slack message (brief, friendly).
```

Consistency Across Multiple Outputs

When you need Copilot to generate multiple pieces that feel like they belong together — chapters of a document, a series of emails, a set of product descriptions — consistency is key.

Establish a Template First

```
I need to write descriptions for 10 products. Here is the format each descriptio
n should follow:

Product Name:
Tagline: (under 10 words, punchy)
Description: (exactly 50 words, benefit-focused)
Key Features: (3 bullet points)
Price: (include currency)

Here is the first product: [details]
```

Once Copilot produces the first one and you approve the style, say:

```
Perfect. Now do the same for the next product: [details]
```

Style Anchoring

If you notice Copilot drifting from the established style, anchor it back:

```
The last description was more formal than the first two. Match the tone of the f
irst description – casual, punchy, benefit-focused.
```

Exporting and Sharing Results

Getting content out of Copilot and into your actual work is the last step in the formatting chain.

Copy and Paste

The simplest method. In the Copilot web interface, copy responses using the copy button that appears when you hover. Tables, lists, and formatted text copy cleanly into Word, Google Docs, and email clients.

Copilot in Microsoft 365 Apps

When you use Copilot inside Word, Excel, PowerPoint, or Outlook, the output is already in the right format. This is the most seamless workflow and one of the strongest reasons to use Copilot within the Microsoft ecosystem rather than the standalone chat.

Copilot Pages

For content you want to collaborate on or refine further, save Copilot output to a Page. Pages preserve formatting and let you keep editing with AI assistance. They are especially useful for content multiple people will review.

Markdown Awareness

Copilot's chat output uses Markdown — headers with # symbols, bold with double asterisks, tables with pipe characters. In a Markdown-aware editor (Notion, GitHub, many CMS platforms), the formatting renders correctly. In plain text environments, you may need to strip the syntax.

Quick Reference: Format Instructions

Here is a cheat sheet of formatting instructions you can append to almost any prompt:

What You Want	What to Say
A table	"Present as a table with columns for [X], [Y], [Z]"
Bullet points	"Format as bullet points"
Numbered steps	"Give me numbered steps"
Specific length	"Keep it under [N] words" or "Exactly [N] paragraphs"
Formal tone	"Use a formal, professional tone"
Casual tone	"Write in a casual, conversational tone"
For email	"Format this as an email with subject line"
For slides	"Create as slide content with bullet points under 10 words each"

What You Want	What to Say
Comparison	"Compare as a table with [criteria] columns"
Summary first	"Start with a one-sentence summary, then provide details"

Formatting is not an afterthought. It is part of the prompt. Include at least one formatting instruction in every prompt, and Copilot's output shifts from "interesting but I need to rework it" to "I can use this right now."

Part VI: Copilot for Every Audience

"Precision of communication is important, more important than ever, in our era of hair trigger balances."

— Allen Ginsberg

Chapter 22: Copilot for Students and Educators

Few groups stand to benefit more from AI assistants than students and educators — and few face more complicated questions about when and how to use them. Copilot is not just another study tool. It is reshaping how people learn, how teachers teach, and how institutions think about academic integrity.

This chapter is for both sides of the classroom. If you are a student, you will learn how to use Copilot to genuinely enhance your learning — not as a shortcut that undermines it. If you are an educator, you will learn how to integrate Copilot into your teaching, set appropriate boundaries, and prepare students for a world where AI literacy is no longer optional.

How Students Can Use Copilot for Learning

The most important principle for students using Copilot: use it to understand, not to avoid understanding. That difference determines whether Copilot makes you smarter or makes you dependent.

Copilot as a Study Partner

One of the best uses of Copilot is as a tireless study partner that explains concepts in whatever way helps you understand them.

Ask for explanations at your level: > Explain the difference between mitosis and meiosis like I am a visual learner who struggles with biology. Use an analogy that involves something from everyday life.

Request multiple explanations: > I still do not understand the Krebs cycle. Explain it three different ways: first as a simple analogy, then as a step-by-step process, then as a summary I could put on a flashcard.

Test your understanding: > I think the French Revolution happened because of food shortages. Am I on the right track? What am I missing? Do not just give me the answer — help me think through it.

That last prompt is the key. When you ask Copilot to help you think rather than think for you, it becomes a genuine learning tool.

Creating Study Materials

Copilot excels at generating study materials tailored to your specific needs.

Flashcards: > Create 20 flashcards for my AP Chemistry exam on chemical bonding. Format: Question on one line, answer on the next. Include ionic, covalent, and metallic bonding. Mix conceptual questions with practice problems.

Practice Quizzes: > Write a 15-question practice quiz on Chapter 7 of my U.S. History textbook (the Civil War era). Mix question types: 5 multiple choice, 5 true/false, and 5 short answer. Include an answer key at the end.

Summary Sheets: > Summarize the key concepts from my statistics course on hypothesis testing. Organize it as a one-page study sheet with definitions, formulas, decision rules, and one worked example for each type of test.

Getting Unstuck on Homework

There is a right way and a wrong way.

Wrong way: "Solve problem 14 from page 203." **Right way:** "I am stuck on a calculus problem that asks me to find the derivative of x^3 * sin(x). I know I need to use the product rule, but I am getting confused about which function is f and which is g. Can you walk me through the setup without giving me the final answer?"

The wrong way gives you an answer you cannot explain. The right way teaches you the process so you can solve similar problems yourself.

Another good approach: > I solved this problem and got 42, but the answer key says 38. Here is my work: [show work]. Where did I go wrong?

Having Copilot identify your specific error is far more educational than having it do the problem from scratch.

Writing Assistance (Not Writing Replacement)

Students often need help with the writing process — and there is a real difference between getting writing help and having something written for you.

Appropriate uses: - "Here is my thesis statement. Is it specific enough, or is it too broad?" - "I wrote this paragraph arguing that renewable energy is cost-effective. Does my reasoning have any logical gaps?" - "Suggest three ways I could strengthen the conclusion of this essay." - "Check this paragraph for grammar and clarity. Explain any changes you suggest so I can learn from them."

Inappropriate use: - "Write a 1,000-word essay on the causes of World War I."

The line is clear: Copilot should help you become a better writer, not replace you as the writer.

Learning New Skills

Copilot is an excellent tutor for skill acquisition — a programming language, a musical concept, a new language, or a professional skill.

> I want to learn basic Python programming. I have never coded before. Create a learning plan that takes me from complete beginner to being able to write simple programs in 30 days. Break it into daily sessions of about 30 minutes each.

Work through the plan step by step, asking Copilot to explain concepts, generate practice exercises, and review your attempts.

Homework Help vs. Academic Integrity

This is the most important section in the chapter, because it addresses the question every student, parent, and educator is asking: where is the line?

The Core Principle

Academic integrity policies exist because the point of assignments is learning. When you submit AI-generated work as your own, you are not just breaking a rule — you are cheating yourself out of the learning the assignment was designed to produce.

Think of fitness. If you hire someone to run your miles, you technically "completed" the workout — but your body did not benefit. Using Copilot to do your thinking works the same way.

A Clear Framework

Here is a framework that works for most academic contexts:

Always acceptable: - Using Copilot to understand concepts you are struggling with - Generating practice problems and quizzes - Getting feedback on your own work - Brainstorming ideas (which you then develop yourself) - Checking grammar and clarity on writing you produced - Learning how to use tools and technologies

Usually acceptable (check your institution's policy): - Using Copilot to help outline an essay you will write yourself - Getting help debugging code you wrote - Asking for explanations of feedback you received from a teacher - Using Copilot as a research starting point (with your own verification)

Generally not acceptable: - Having Copilot write essays, papers, or reports that you submit as your own work - Using Copilot to solve homework problems and submitting the answers without doing the work yourself - Copying Copilot's code directly for a programming assignment - Using Copilot during exams where AI tools are not permitted

Always unacceptable: - Submitting AI-generated work and claiming you wrote it yourself - Using Copilot to circumvent plagiarism detection - Using AI tools in assessments that explicitly prohibit them

The Evolving Policy Landscape

Academic integrity policies around AI are evolving fast. What was prohibited in 2024 may be permitted — or required — in 2026. Always check your institution's current AI use policy, and when in doubt, ask your instructor. Most educators appreciate students who clarify the boundaries rather than assume.

Disclosure

When you use AI assistance, disclose it. Many institutions now require or encourage AI disclosures. Even when not required, transparency builds trust. A simple note works: "I used Microsoft Copilot to brainstorm this essay's structure and to check grammar on my final draft. All arguments and analysis are my own."

For Educators: Integrating Copilot into Teaching

If you are an educator, you have probably spent the last couple of years grappling with AI in your classroom. Here is a practical framework for shifting from "how do I prevent students from using this?" to "how do I help students use this well?"

Rethinking Assignment Design

The most effective response to AI is not policing — it is designing assignments that make AI a complement to learning, not a substitute.

Assignments that resist AI shortcuts: - Personal reflection and experience-based writing - Analysis of class discussions or in-person activities - Multi-stage projects where students show their process - Oral presentations and defenses of written work - Collaborative projects with peer accountability - Real-time, in-class writing and problem-solving

Assignments that leverage AI productively: - "Use Copilot to generate a first draft, then critically evaluate and substantially revise it. Submit both versions with a reflection on what you changed and why." - "Have Copilot argue the opposite side of your position. Then strengthen your original argument to address the counterpoints it raised." - "Use Copilot to research a topic, then fact-check its claims. Document which claims were accurate, which were inaccurate, and how you verified them."

These assignments teach critical thinking, information literacy, and AI fluency all at once.

Teaching AI Literacy

Students need to understand how AI works, where it fails, and what its limitations are — not just how to use it. Consider dedicating class time to:

- **How language models work** (at a conceptual level — the prediction mechanism, training data, the difference between "knowing" and "pattern matching")
- **Hallucination demonstrations** (ask Copilot factual questions in your subject area and have students fact-check the answers)
- **Prompt engineering** (teach students to get better results, which is itself a critical thinking exercise)

- **Bias exploration** (have students ask the same question from different perspectives and compare responses)
- **Ethical case studies** (discuss real scenarios involving AI use in professional and academic contexts)

Lesson Planning with Copilot

Copilot saves educators significant time on the administrative and creative side of teaching.

Lesson plan generation: > Create a 50-minute lesson plan for a 10th-grade English class on analyzing symbolism in "The Great Gatsby." Include a warm-up activity, a main instructional segment, a group activity, and an exit ticket. The class has 28 students with mixed reading levels.

Differentiated materials: > Take this reading passage and create three versions: one at grade level, one simplified for struggling readers, and one extended for advanced students. Keep the core content the same.

Assessment creation: > Write a rubric for a persuasive essay assignment. Categories: thesis and argument, evidence and support, organization, language and conventions, and counterargument. Four levels for each category: Beginning, Developing, Proficient, Advanced. Include specific descriptors for each cell.

Parent communication: > Draft a parent email explaining our new classroom AI use policy. Tone: informative, reassuring, collaborative. Explain that we are teaching students to use AI responsibly rather than banning it, and describe the guardrails we have in place.

Age-Appropriate Use

AI assistants raise different considerations at different ages.

Elementary School (Ages 5–10)

At this age, Copilot use should be supervised and limited. Appropriate uses include: - A parent or teacher using Copilot to generate reading material at the child's level - Creating simple, fun practice problems - Supervised exploration of asking questions and evaluating answers

Children at this age should not be using AI chat interfaces independently. They lack the critical thinking skills to evaluate AI responses and may develop an unhealthy reliance on instant answers.

Middle School (Ages 11–13)

Students at this age can begin supervised, independent use with clear guidelines: - Learning to fact-check AI responses - Using Copilot for study support (explanations, practice quizzes) - Beginning to learn about how AI works and its limitations - Clear rules about what is and is not acceptable for homework

High School (Ages 14–18)

High school students can use Copilot more independently, with emphasis on: - Responsible use and academic integrity - Critical evaluation of AI output - Using AI as a learning accelerator, not a shortcut - Understanding the professional and ethical dimensions of AI use - Building habits that will serve them in college and careers

College and Beyond

At the post-secondary level, AI fluency is increasingly expected. Students should be able to: - Use AI tools effectively and ethically - Understand the strengths and limitations of AI-generated content - Disclose AI use appropriately - Apply AI tools to enhance their professional capabilities

Copilot in Educational Microsoft 365 Environments

Many educational institutions use Microsoft 365 Education, which includes Copilot features and controls tailored to academic settings.

What Administrators Control

IT administrators in educational environments can: - Enable or disable Copilot features for specific user groups (students, faculty, staff) - Set age-appropriate restrictions - Control whether Copilot can access organizational data - Configure data privacy settings to comply with regulations like FERPA (in the U.S.) and GDPR (in Europe) - Manage which Copilot features are available in which applications

Microsoft 365 Education Plans and Copilot

Copilot availability in educational environments depends on the institution's licensing. Microsoft 365 Education plans include varying levels of Copilot access, and institutions can purchase additional Copilot licenses for faculty and students.

Check with your institution's IT department to learn which features are available and which restrictions apply.

Data Privacy in Education

Educational AI use raises specific data privacy concerns: - Student data is protected by regulations (FERPA, COPPA, GDPR) that apply to AI tools as they do to any other technology - Institutions should have clear policies about what student data can and cannot be shared with AI tools - Students under 18 may have additional protections that affect how AI services can be used

The Bottom Line

Copilot is neither the end of learning nor the salvation of education. It is a powerful tool that, like any tool, can be used well or poorly. Students who use it to deepen understanding will learn faster and develop skills that serve them for decades. Students who use it to avoid learning will find themselves unprepared for a world that demands genuine competence.

Educators who embrace AI thoughtfully — teaching students to use it responsibly while designing assignments that build real skills — prepare students for a workplace where AI is not optional. Those who help students develop the judgment to know when to use AI, when to set it aside, and how to think critically about its output are teaching one of the most important skills of the twenty-first century.

Chapter 23: Copilot for Business and Teams

If you are evaluating Microsoft Copilot for your organization — or already using it and trying to get more value from the investment — this chapter is for you. We will cover the business and enterprise tiers of Microsoft 365 Copilot, how to deploy and govern it across a team or company, practical use cases by department, and how to build an AI usage policy that balances productivity with risk.

We will also address the question that comes up in every leadership conversation: how does Copilot compare to the alternatives?

Microsoft 365 Copilot for Business: What You Get

Microsoft 365 Copilot for Business is not the same product as free Copilot or the consumer Microsoft 365 plans (Personal, Family, Premium). It is a deeply integrated AI layer that sits inside the Microsoft 365 applications your organization already uses — Word, Excel, PowerPoint, Outlook, Teams, and more.

Business Plans

Microsoft offers two primary business tiers:

Microsoft 365 Copilot for Business ($18–21/user/month): For small and medium businesses. Adds Copilot capabilities to Microsoft 365 Business Standard or Business Premium subscriptions. Users get AI assistance in Word, Excel, PowerPoint, Outlook, Teams, and the Copilot chat experience with access to organizational data through Microsoft Graph.

Microsoft 365 Copilot Enterprise ($30/user/month): For large organizations with advanced security, compliance, and governance needs. Includes everything in the business plan plus enterprise-grade data protection, customization through Copilot Studio, advanced usage analytics, and integration with enterprise data sources.

Both tiers require an underlying Microsoft 365 subscription. Copilot is an add-on, not a standalone product.

What Business Copilot Can Do That Consumer Copilot Cannot

The defining feature of Microsoft 365 Copilot for Business is its connection to your organizational data through Microsoft Graph. That is what makes it fundamentally different from the consumer product.

When a business user asks Copilot a question, it does not just draw on training data and web search. It can also reference:

- **Emails** in the user's mailbox
- **Documents** in SharePoint and OneDrive
- **Meeting transcripts** and chat history in Teams
- **Calendar** events and scheduling data
- **Contacts** and organizational charts
- **Files** shared within the organization

You can ask "summarize the key decisions from last week's product team meetings" or "find the latest version of the Q3 marketing budget" and Copilot will search your organizational data to answer.

This is both the greatest strength and the greatest responsibility of business Copilot. It is powerful precisely because it can access your organization's data — which makes data governance and permissions matter more than ever.

Deploying Copilot Across Your Organization

Rolling out Copilot is not like installing a new app. It is change management — planning, governance, and ongoing attention.

Pre-Deployment Checklist

Before enabling Copilot for your organization, address these items:

1. Data hygiene. Copilot only surfaces data the user already has permission to access. If your SharePoint permissions are messy — if people have access to files they should not — Copilot will surface those files. Clean up permissions before deployment.

2. Licensing. Determine which users need Copilot licenses. Not everyone needs one. Start with power users who live in Microsoft 365 and will see immediate value.

3. Security review. Ensure your organization meets Microsoft's security requirements for Copilot: Multi-Factor Authentication (MFA), conditional access policies, and data loss prevention (DLP) configurations.

4. Policy development. Create or update your AI usage policy before users start experimenting. We cover this in detail later.

5. Training plan. Budget time for training. Users who receive Copilot without guidance underutilize it. A small training investment pays significant returns.

Phased Rollout Strategy

Most successful deployments follow a phased approach:

Phase 1: Pilot group (4–6 weeks). Pick 20–50 enthusiastic users across departments. These early adopters discover use cases, surface issues, and become internal champions.

Phase 2: Department expansion (4–8 weeks). Based on pilot feedback, expand to entire departments where Copilot showed the most value. Refine training materials and governance based on what you learned.

Phase 3: Broad deployment. Roll out to the rest of the organization with mature policies, training resources, and support in place.

Phase 4: Optimization. Monitor usage analytics, gather feedback, and identify new use cases. Copilot adoption is not a one-time event — it is ongoing.

Admin Controls and Governance

Microsoft provides administrators with extensive controls over Copilot:

- **User-level control:** Enable or disable Copilot for specific users or groups
- **App-level control:** Enable Copilot in some Microsoft 365 apps but not others
- **Data access controls:** Configure which data sources Copilot can access

- **Sensitivity labels:** Copilot respects Microsoft Information Protection labels, so classified or restricted documents remain protected
- **Usage analytics:** Monitor adoption rates, common use cases, and identify where additional training is needed
- **Copilot Studio:** Create custom Copilot agents and plugins tailored to your organization's specific workflows

Use Cases by Department

Copilot's value varies by function. Here is a department-by-department guide to the highest-impact use cases.

Sales

- **Meeting preparation:** "Summarize all recent email exchanges with [prospect name] and highlight any concerns they have raised."
- **Proposal drafting:** Use Copilot in Word to draft proposals that reference previous successful proposals and incorporate prospect-specific details.
- **CRM updates:** Copilot can help draft call summaries and follow-up emails immediately after customer interactions.
- **Pipeline analysis:** In Excel, ask Copilot to analyze your sales data and identify trends, at-risk deals, or opportunities.

Marketing

- **Content creation:** Draft blog posts, social media content, email campaigns, and ad copy.
- **Campaign analysis:** Ask Copilot to analyze campaign performance data in Excel and identify what is working.
- **Competitive research:** Use Copilot chat with web search to research competitor activities and market trends.
- **Brand consistency:** Provide brand guidelines in your prompt and ask Copilot to ensure all content adheres to them.

Human Resources

- **Job descriptions:** Draft job postings based on role requirements, adjusting for tone and inclusivity.

- **Policy documents:** Create or update HR policies with Copilot in Word.
- **Employee communications:** Draft announcements, newsletters, and sensitive communications with appropriate tone.
- **Interview preparation:** Generate interview questions tailored to specific roles and competency frameworks.
- **Onboarding materials:** Create orientation documents and training guides.

Finance

- **Report generation:** Use Copilot in Excel to analyze financial data and generate summary reports.
- **Budget analysis:** Ask Copilot to compare budget versus actual spending and highlight variances.
- **Presentation creation:** Turn financial data into executive-ready PowerPoint presentations.
- **Compliance documentation:** Draft compliance reports and audit preparation materials.

Operations

- **Process documentation:** Use Copilot to create standard operating procedures based on verbal descriptions.
- **Meeting efficiency:** Leverage Copilot in Teams to summarize meetings, track action items, and generate follow-up emails.
- **Project status reports:** Create weekly status updates that pull from emails, Teams chats, and project documents.
- **Vendor communications:** Draft RFPs, vendor evaluations, and contract summaries.

IT

- **Documentation:** Generate technical documentation, user guides, and knowledge base articles.
- **Incident response:** Draft incident reports and post-mortem analyses.
- **Change management:** Create change request documents and impact analyses.

- **Help desk support:** Build FAQ documents and troubleshooting guides for common issues.

Executive Leadership

- **Strategic analysis:** Ask Copilot to analyze market data, internal performance metrics, and competitive intelligence.
- **Board materials:** Prepare board presentations and executive briefings from internal data.
- **Communication:** Draft all-hands announcements, investor updates, and strategic memos.
- **Decision support:** Use Think Deeper for complex decisions that involve multiple variables and trade-offs.

Building a Company AI Usage Policy

Every organization using Copilot needs an AI usage policy. Without one you get inconsistent behavior, potential data leaks, and employees who either over-rely on AI or refuse to use it.

What Your Policy Should Cover

1. Approved tools. Specify which AI tools are approved for business use. If Copilot is the sanctioned tool, say so — and explain why (data protection, enterprise controls, integration with existing systems).

2. Acceptable use cases. List tasks where AI use is encouraged, permitted, or prohibited. Be specific. "You may use Copilot to draft internal emails and meeting summaries. You may not use Copilot to generate content for regulatory filings without legal review."

3. Data handling. Define what data can and cannot be shared with AI tools. Customer PII? Financial data? Trade secrets? Attorney-client privileged information? Be explicit.

4. Quality control. Require human review of all AI-generated content before it is sent externally, published, or used for decision-making. AI output is a draft, never a final product.

5. Disclosure. Set expectations for when AI use should be disclosed. This varies by context — internal documents may not require disclosure, but client-facing materials might.

6. Intellectual property. Address ownership of AI-generated content and any copyright considerations relevant to your industry.

7. Bias and fairness. Acknowledge that AI tools can reflect biases and require human judgment — especially in hiring, performance reviews, and customer interactions.

8. Training requirements. Specify what training employees must complete before using AI tools.

Sample Policy Framework

Here is a condensed framework you can adapt:

> **[Company Name] AI Usage Policy**
>
> **Purpose:** This policy establishes guidelines for the responsible use of AI tools in our organization.
>
> **Approved tools:** Microsoft 365 Copilot is the approved AI assistant for business use. Employees should not use personal AI accounts (such as free ChatGPT or Claude) for work-related tasks, as these lack enterprise data protections.
>
> **Permitted uses:** Drafting content, analyzing data, summarizing information, brainstorming, research, and meeting support.
>
> **Prohibited uses:** Generating content for regulatory or legal filings without expert review; sharing customer PII, trade secrets, or confidential financial data in prompts outside of approved enterprise tools; using AI to make automated decisions about employees or customers without human oversight.
>
> **Quality control:** All AI-generated content must be reviewed by a human before external distribution. Employees are responsible for the accuracy and appropriateness of any content they produce with AI assistance.
>
> **Training:** All employees with Copilot licenses must complete AI awareness training within 30 days of receiving access.

Measuring ROI

Leadership will ask whether Copilot is worth the investment. Here is how to measure it.

Quantitative Metrics

- **Time saved per user per week:** Survey users on time saved on routine tasks. Even 30 minutes per week across 100 users is significant.
- **Adoption rate:** What percentage of licensed users are actively using Copilot? Low adoption means wasted licenses or inadequate training.
- **Task completion time:** For specific workflows (meeting summaries, report generation, email drafting), compare before and after.

Qualitative Metrics

- **Employee satisfaction:** Are employees finding Copilot valuable? Would they want to keep it if the license were up for renewal?
- **Quality of output:** Are reports, emails, and presentations improving in quality?
- **Cross-department collaboration:** Is Copilot helping break down information silos?

Cost-Benefit Calculation

A rough formula: a user with a fully loaded cost of $75/hour who saves 30 minutes per week using Copilot generates roughly $150/month in productivity value — well above the $18–30/month license cost. The math works even with conservative estimates.

Copilot vs. Competitors for Business Use

Organizations often ask: should we use Microsoft Copilot, or would ChatGPT Team, Claude for Enterprise, or Google Gemini for Workspace fit better?

Microsoft 365 Copilot

Best for: Organizations already deep in the Microsoft ecosystem. The integration with Word, Excel, PowerPoint, Outlook, and Teams is unmatched. If your team lives in Microsoft 365, Copilot meets them where they already work.

Strengths: Deep Microsoft 365 integration, organizational data access through Microsoft Graph, enterprise security and compliance, familiar interface.

Weaknesses: Requires Microsoft 365 subscription, costs add up at scale, some features still maturing.

ChatGPT Enterprise/Team

Best for: Organizations that want a versatile AI assistant not tied to any specific productivity suite. ChatGPT excels in creative tasks, coding, and open-ended problem solving.

Strengths: Powerful general-purpose AI, strong coding capabilities, custom GPTs, Agent Mode for complex tasks, broad plugin ecosystem.

Weaknesses: No native integration with Microsoft 365, separate interface from daily workflow tools.

Claude for Enterprise

Best for: Organizations that prioritize long-document analysis, careful reasoning, and nuanced writing. Claude excels in scenarios requiring deep analysis and tends to be more cautious and thoughtful in its responses.

Strengths: Excellent writing quality, strong analytical reasoning, large context window, careful handling of sensitive topics.

Weaknesses: Smaller feature ecosystem than ChatGPT, no native productivity suite integration.

Google Gemini for Workspace

Best for: Organizations using Google Workspace (Gmail, Google Docs, Google Sheets, Google Slides). Gemini integrates with Workspace the way Copilot integrates with Microsoft 365.

Strengths: Native Google Workspace integration, strong at research and information synthesis, competitive pricing.

Weaknesses: Less mature than Copilot in some enterprise features, smaller market share in enterprise environments.

The Practical Answer

For most organizations already on Microsoft 365, Copilot is the natural choice. The integration advantage is real — AI inside the tools you already use every day is fundamentally more useful than AI in a separate tab. For specialized needs — advanced coding, long-document analysis, creative work — supplementing Copilot with ChatGPT or Claude can make sense.

The companion titles in the Finnoybu Press library — *ChatGPT: The Definitive Guide*, *Claude: The Definitive Guide*, and *Gemini: The Complete Guide* — provide comprehensive coverage of each platform if you want to evaluate them in depth.

Chapter 24: Copilot for Developers

When most people hear "Microsoft Copilot," they picture the AI assistant in Word, Excel, and Teams. For developers, Copilot means something different — and in many ways, more transformative: GitHub Copilot, the AI coding assistant that has fundamentally changed how software is written.

GitHub Copilot is arguably where Microsoft's AI ambitions started. Launched in 2021, it was one of the first commercial applications of large language models, and it has since become the most widely adopted AI coding tool in the world. If you write code for a living — or even occasionally — this chapter shows what GitHub Copilot can do, how to use it well, and how it fits alongside other developer AI tools.

What Is GitHub Copilot?

GitHub Copilot is an AI-powered coding assistant that integrates directly into your code editor. It watches what you type, understands the context of your code, and offers suggestions — from single-line completions to entire functions — in real time. Think of it as an extremely knowledgeable pair programmer who never gets tired, never gets frustrated, and has read virtually every public code repository on the internet.

Copilot is more than an autocomplete engine. It can:

- **Complete code** as you type, predicting what comes next
- **Generate functions** from natural language descriptions
- **Chat about code** — answer questions, explain code, suggest improvements
- **Debug** by analyzing error messages and suggesting fixes
- **Write tests** based on your existing code
- **Refactor** code for better structure, readability, or performance
- **Translate** between programming languages
- **Generate documentation** from code

It works across dozens of programming languages, with particularly strong support for Python, JavaScript, TypeScript, Java, C#, Go, Ruby, and Rust.

GitHub Copilot Tiers

GitHub Copilot offers five tiers, each designed for different users and organizations.

Free ($0/month)

The Free tier gives individual developers a taste of Copilot at no cost:

- 2,000 code completions per month (the figure that has been in place since the December 2024 launch)
- 50 chat messages per month
- Access in VS Code and on GitHub.com
- Limited model selection

Enough for hobbyists, students, and developers evaluating the tool before committing. 2,000 completions per month sounds like a lot, but active developers can burn through it in a week or two.

Heads-up: billing model change. Beginning June 1, 2026, all GitHub Copilot plans transition to usage-based billing with monthly AI Credits, replacing the fixed-allowance approach above. The exact Free-tier credit allotment is being announced on a rolling basis — check github.com/features/copilot for current numbers before you plan around them.

Pro ($10/month)

The Pro tier is for individual professional developers:

- Unlimited code completions
- Unlimited chat messages
- Multi-model support (GPT-5.4, Claude, Gemini)
- Copilot in VS Code, Visual Studio, JetBrains IDEs, Neovim, and Xcode
- Copilot in the CLI (command-line interface)

For most individual developers, Pro is the sweet spot. Unlimited completions alone justify the cost if you code regularly.

Pro+ ($39/month)

Pro+ adds premium features for developers who want the absolute best:

- Everything in Pro
- Access to the most capable models with higher rate limits
- Copilot for pull request summaries on GitHub
- Advanced agent capabilities
- Priority access to new features

Pro+ is worth it for developers who lean heavily on AI assistance throughout their workflow and want frontier model capabilities.

Business ($19/user/month)

The Business tier is for teams and organizations:

- Everything in Pro
- Organization-wide management and policy controls
- IP indemnification (legal protection for code generated by Copilot)
- Admin controls for enabling/disabling features
- Usage analytics and audit logs
- Code referencing filters (block suggestions matching public code)
- SAML SSO and SCIM provisioning

IP indemnification matters for businesses concerned about the legal status of AI-generated code. Microsoft assumes the legal risk for any intellectual property claims arising from code generated by Copilot in the Business tier.

Enterprise ($39/user/month)

Enterprise includes everything in Business plus:

- Fine-tuned models on your organization's codebase
- Bing search integration for code context
- Knowledge bases for organizational documentation

- Advanced security features
- Compliance and data residency controls

Enterprise is for large organizations with significant codebases, strict compliance requirements, and a need to tune Copilot to their specific technology stack.

Multi-Model Support

One of the most significant developments in GitHub Copilot is multi-model support. Rather than locking you into a single AI model, Copilot now lets you choose between multiple models depending on the task.

Available Models

- **GPT-5.4:** Microsoft and OpenAI's flagship model. Strong general-purpose coding, excellent instruction following, good at understanding complex codebases.
- **Claude:** Anthropic's model (Sonnet or Opus, depending on the tier). Excels at careful reasoning, long code analysis, and producing well-structured, readable code. Many developers prefer Claude for complex refactoring and architectural decisions.
- **Gemini:** Google's model. Strong at multi-language tasks, research-oriented coding, and diverse tech stacks.

Choosing the Right Model

There is no single "best" model — it depends on the task:

- **Quick completions and boilerplate:** Any model works. GPT-5.4 tends to be fastest.
- **Complex logic and algorithms:** Claude and GPT-5.4 both excel. Try both and see which produces cleaner results for your language and domain.
- **Understanding large codebases:** Claude's large context window makes it strong at reasoning across large files or multiple files at once.
- **Documentation and explanation:** Claude tends to produce the most thorough and well-organized explanations.
- **Rapid prototyping:** GPT-5.4 is often fastest at generating working code.

In practice, most developers settle on one model for most tasks and switch for specific situations. The beauty of multi-model support is experimenting without switching tools.

Copilot in Your IDE

Most developers use GitHub Copilot inside their code editor. Here is how it works in the most popular environments.

VS Code

VS Code has the deepest Copilot integration of any editor. After installing the GitHub Copilot extension:

- **Inline completions** appear as ghost text as you type. Press Tab to accept, Escape to dismiss.
- **Copilot Chat** opens as a sidebar panel where you can ask questions about your code, request changes, or get explanations.
- **Inline chat** (Ctrl+I or Cmd+I) lets you ask Copilot a question right in your editor, at the cursor position.
- **Terminal integration** helps with command-line tasks.
- **Agent mode** lets Copilot make multi-file edits, run commands, and iterate on changes autonomously.

Visual Studio

Copilot in Visual Studio offers similar capabilities with tight integration into the .NET ecosystem. For C# or .NET developers, the Visual Studio experience is excellent.

JetBrains IDEs

IntelliJ IDEA, PyCharm, WebStorm, and other JetBrains products support Copilot through a plugin. Inline completions and chat are included, though some features arrive later than in VS Code.

Neovim and Other Editors

Copilot has plugins for Neovim, Vim, and other editors, offering inline completions. The experience is more minimal than VS Code but functional for developers who live in these environments.

Getting the Most from GitHub Copilot

Installing Copilot and letting it autocomplete is like buying a sports car and only driving it in parking lots. Here are techniques for extracting maximum value.

Write Comments First

One of the most effective Copilot techniques is writing a comment describing what you want, then letting Copilot generate the code:

```
# Function that takes a list of transactions and returns
# the total amount grouped by category, sorted by total
# descending. Skip transactions with negative amounts.
```

Copilot will often generate the complete function from a comment like this. The clearer your comment, the better the code.

Be Specific in Chat

When using Copilot Chat, the prompting fundamentals from Chapter 19 apply:

- **Vague:** "Fix this function."
- **Specific:** "This function is supposed to handle pagination but it returns duplicate results when the page size does not evenly divide the total count. Fix the off-by-one error in the offset calculation."

Use Context Strategically

Copilot's suggestions are shaped by the code around the cursor. If you want Copilot to generate code in a particular style, keep examples of that style nearby — in the same file or in open tabs (in VS Code, Copilot can reference open files for context).

Review Everything

This bears repeating: never blindly accept Copilot's suggestions. AI-generated code can contain:

- Subtle logical errors
- Security vulnerabilities (SQL injection, improper input validation)
- Outdated API usage
- Inefficient implementations
- Code that works but violates your team's conventions

Treat Copilot output like code from a fast new team member who needs code review. Read, understand, and test before committing.

Iterate with Chat

When Copilot's first attempt misses, use chat to refine:

- "This is close, but use async/await instead of callbacks."
- "Good structure, but add error handling for the API call."
- "Refactor this to use the repository pattern."

When to Use GitHub Copilot vs. Alternatives

The developer AI landscape has expanded. GitHub Copilot is one option among several — knowing when to use which tool helps you work more effectively.

GitHub Copilot

Best for: Real-time coding assistance inside your IDE. Copilot is unmatched for inline completions — AI suggesting code as you type, seamless and fast. The best tool for the moment-to-moment flow of writing code.

Claude Code

Best for: Complex, multi-file tasks requiring understanding of your entire codebase. Claude Code operates at the project level — reading file structure, understanding architectural patterns, making coordinated changes across multiple files, and running terminal commands. For refactoring an entire module, setting up a new project, or debugging an issue that spans multiple files, Claude Code is the more capable tool.

For comprehensive coverage of Claude Code, see the companion Finnoybu Press title *Claude Code: The Power User Guide.*

ChatGPT

Best for: General-purpose coding questions, learning new technologies, exploring architectural options, and working through complex problems conversationally. ChatGPT's Agent Mode can write and execute code in a sandboxed environment.

The Practical Stack

Many professional developers use multiple tools:

- **GitHub Copilot** for inline completions and quick in-editor assistance
- **Claude Code** (or a similar agentic coding tool) for larger refactoring, debugging, and multi-file tasks
- **ChatGPT or Claude** in a browser for architectural discussions, learning, and exploratory coding

These tools complement each other rather than replace each other. The key is matching the tool to the task.

Getting Started

If you are new to GitHub Copilot, here is how to get up and running:

1. **Sign up** at github.com/features/copilot. Choose your tier (start with Free if you want to evaluate first).
2. **Install the extension** in your code editor (search for "GitHub Copilot" in the extensions marketplace).
3. **Sign in** with your GitHub account.
4. **Start coding.** Copilot begins suggesting completions immediately.
5. **Open Copilot Chat** to ask questions about your code.
6. **Experiment with models** on Pro or higher — try the same task with different models and compare results.

The learning curve is gentle. Most developers feel comfortable within a day or two and see significant productivity gains within a week. The key is to resist accepting every suggestion uncritically — the developers who get the most from Copilot use it as a collaborator, not a crutch.

Part VII: Using AI Responsibly

"The best way to predict your future is to create it."

— Peter Drucker

Chapter 25: What Copilot Gets Wrong

Every chapter so far has shown what Copilot can do. This one is about what it cannot do — or more precisely, what it does badly. Understanding Copilot's failure modes is not pessimism. It is the difference between using a powerful tool wisely and trusting it blindly.

Copilot is impressive. It is also wrong more often than most people realize, in ways that are sometimes obvious and sometimes dangerously subtle. To use Copilot productively and safely, you need to know where the guardrails end.

Hallucinations

The single most important limitation of Copilot — and every AI assistant built on large language models — is hallucination. Hallucination is when the AI generates information that sounds plausible, is delivered with full confidence, and is entirely fabricated.

What Hallucination Looks Like

Copilot might:

- **Invent citations.** It may reference a study in the *Journal of Applied Psychology* by Dr. Sarah Chen in 2023 — and none of it is real. The journal exists, but the study and author do not.
- **Create fake statistics.** "According to a 2025 McKinsey survey, 73% of companies have adopted AI tools." The number, the survey, or both may be fabricated.
- **Fabricate details about real things.** It may describe a real company's product but attribute features that do not exist.
- **Confidently misstate facts.** It may say a specific law was passed in a specific year when it was passed in a different year, or never passed at all.

Why Hallucination Happens

Large language models do not look up facts. They generate text by predicting the most likely next word from patterns they learned during training. When the model does not "know" something, it does not say "I don't know." It generates the most plausible-sounding text it can — which may or may not be accurate.

This is not a bug that will be fixed in the next update. It is a fundamental characteristic of how these models work. Hallucination rates are dropping, and Copilot's Bing Search grounding helps by anchoring responses to real web sources. But hallucination has not been eliminated and will not be for some time.

How to Protect Yourself

Verify independently. Any factual claim that matters — a statistic, a date, a name, a legal requirement — should be verified through a reliable source. Copilot's citations are a starting point, but check that the source actually says what Copilot claims.

Be skeptical of specificity. The more specific and detailed Copilot's answer, the more carefully you should verify it. Specific details (exact percentages, study authors, precise dates) are where hallucination is most likely.

Ask for sources. When Copilot makes a factual claim, ask for sources. If it cannot provide them, or the sources do not check out, treat the claim as unverified.

Use Think Deeper for factual questions. Extended reasoning tends to be more cautious and accurate than quick responses, though it is not immune to hallucination.

Knowledge Limitations

Copilot's knowledge has boundaries. Understanding them helps you avoid errors.

Training Data Cutoffs

Like all language models, Copilot's underlying model was trained on data up to a certain date. Events, products, laws, and developments after that date are not part of its training. Bing Search grounding mitigates this — Copilot can search the web for current information — but only when the search is triggered and the information is available online.

Depth vs. Breadth

Copilot has broad knowledge across many topics but varies significantly in depth. It knows a lot about popular programming languages but less about obscure ones. It can discuss major legal principles but is unreliable on jurisdiction-specific details. It understands common business concepts but struggles with highly specialized industry knowledge.

The rule: the more niche or specialized the topic, the less reliable Copilot's responses become. If you are asking about something only a handful of experts truly understand, verify everything.

Local and Recent Information

Copilot can search the web for recent and local information, but its search is not perfect. It may miss very recent developments, local news, or information that is not well-represented online. For time-sensitive or location-specific questions, cross-reference.

Math and Reasoning Errors

This one surprises people. Copilot can explain complex mathematical concepts clearly, generate formulas, walk through problem-solving steps — and still arrive at the wrong answer.

Arithmetic Mistakes

Language models sometimes make basic arithmetic errors. They may correctly set up a multi-step calculation and then slip on one of the steps. These models process numbers as text patterns, not mathematical values. They are getting better with each generation, but errors still occur.

Logic Errors

Copilot can make logical errors in multi-step reasoning:

- Circular reasoning (using the conclusion as a premise)
- False equivalences (treating two different things as the same)
- Cherry-picking evidence (selecting data that supports a conclusion while ignoring contradictory data)

- Incorrect conditional reasoning (confusing "if A then B" with "if B then A")

These errors are dangerous because Copilot's reasoning often looks correct on the surface. You have to follow the logic step by step to catch them.

Statistical Reasoning

Copilot frequently struggles with:

- Probability calculations, especially conditional probability
- Distinguishing correlation from causation
- Understanding sampling bias
- Interpreting statistical significance correctly

If you are making decisions based on data analysis, double-check Copilot's statistical conclusions. Verify calculations in Excel, Python, or a dedicated statistical tool.

What to Do

For any math or data task where accuracy matters, use Copilot to set up the approach and explain the methodology, then verify calculations independently. In Excel, use Copilot to generate formulas, then spot-check the results with manual calculations on a few data points.

Bias

AI models are trained on human-generated text, and that text reflects the biases of the humans who wrote it and the societies they lived in.

Types of Bias in Copilot

Cultural bias. Copilot's training data is disproportionately English-language and Western. It may present Western perspectives as universal, overlook non-Western viewpoints, or apply American assumptions to questions about other countries.

Gender bias. When asked to generate content about certain professions, Copilot may default to gendered assumptions — describing nurses as "she" and engineers as "he," for example. Microsoft has worked to reduce these biases, but they have not been eliminated.

Confirmation bias. Copilot tends to agree with the framing of your question. Ask "why is remote work better than office work?" and it will argue for remote work. Ask the reverse and it will argue the opposite. This is sometimes called sycophancy — the tendency to tell you what you want to hear.

Recency bias in search. When using web search, Copilot may over-index on recent articles and underweight older but more authoritative sources.

Mitigating Bias

- Ask for multiple perspectives explicitly: "Give me arguments both for and against this position."
- Question one-sided answers: "What would someone who disagrees with this say?"
- Be aware of how your question's framing influences the answer.
- For important decisions, seek out human expertise in addition to AI input.

How to Spot and Handle Errors

The most dangerous Copilot errors are the ones you miss. Here is a practical framework for catching them.

The Confidence Trap

Copilot always sounds confident. The tone is identical whether it is giving you a verified fact or a hallucination. Unlike a human expert, who might say "I'm not sure" or "if I remember correctly," Copilot rarely hedges. You cannot use its confidence as a signal of accuracy.

Train yourself to ignore the confident tone and evaluate the content on its own merits.

Red Flags to Watch For

- **Very specific numbers without context.** "Studies show that 67.3% of companies prefer..." — where did that number come from?

- **Unfamiliar sources or authors.** If Copilot cites a study or expert you have never heard of, verify they exist.
- **Too-perfect answers.** If the answer is unusually comprehensive, neatly organized, and tells you exactly what you wanted to hear, double-check it. Reality is messy.
- **Answers that contradict earlier answers.** In a long conversation, Copilot may shift positions without acknowledging it.
- **Technical claims in unfamiliar domains.** If you are not an expert in the topic, you are less likely to catch errors. Be extra cautious.

A Practical Verification Process

1. **Identify the key claims.** What are the most important factual assertions in Copilot's response?
2. **Assess risk.** What happens if this claim is wrong? A wrong fun fact is low-risk. A wrong legal interpretation is high-risk.
3. **Verify high-risk claims.** Use authoritative sources — official websites, peer-reviewed research, industry publications, professional experts.
4. **Test reasoning.** For analytical responses, follow the logic step by step. Does each step actually support the next?
5. **Seek contradictory evidence.** Ask Copilot "What are the strongest arguments against what you just told me?" or search independently for opposing viewpoints.

The Right Mindset

The right mindset for using Copilot is neither trust nor distrust. It is *verify*. Think of Copilot as a brilliant research assistant who works fast and covers a lot of ground — but whose work needs checking before you stake anything important on it.

That does not mean verifying every word of a casual brainstorm. Match scrutiny to stakes. A creative writing exercise? Take it at face value. A financial analysis going to your board? Check every number.

What Copilot Itself Says About Its Limitations

Ask Copilot about its own limitations and you will get a generally accurate, refreshingly honest answer. It will tell you it can make mistakes, that it should not be your sole source of information for important decisions, and that its responses should be verified.

Take it at its word. The tool itself is telling you not to trust it blindly. That is good advice.

Chapter 26: Privacy, Security, and Safe Use

Every time you type a message to Copilot, you are sharing information with an AI system operated by Microsoft. For a casual question about dinner recipes, the privacy implications are minimal. Once you start using Copilot for work — drafting sensitive emails, analyzing financial data, discussing personnel issues, brainstorming competitive strategy — what happens to your data becomes critical.

This chapter lays out what Microsoft collects, how different Copilot tiers handle your data, what protections exist for business and enterprise users, and how to use Copilot safely in various contexts. No fear-mongering, no hand-waving — just the facts you need to make informed decisions.

What Microsoft Collects

When you use Copilot, Microsoft processes several types of data. Understanding the categories helps you make smart decisions about what you share.

Prompts and Responses

Your prompts and Copilot's responses are processed by Microsoft's AI systems. What happens to this data after processing depends on your tier.

Usage Data

Microsoft collects telemetry about how you use Copilot: which features you use, how often, error logs, and performance metrics. This is similar to telemetry collected by most software products and is used to improve the service.

Account Information

Your Microsoft account information (name, email, subscription tier) is associated with your Copilot usage for billing, authentication, and service delivery.

Files and Documents

If you upload files, paste document content into prompts, or use Copilot within Microsoft 365 apps that access your files, that content is processed by the AI. In Microsoft 365 Copilot for Business, Copilot can also access your organizational data through Microsoft Graph — emails, documents, meeting transcripts, and more.

Data Handling by Tier

Not all Copilot users get the same data protections. Your tier determines how your data is handled.

Free Copilot

With the Free tier:

- Microsoft may use your prompts and responses to improve its AI models (you can opt out in settings)
- Conversations are stored and associated with your Microsoft account
- Standard Microsoft privacy policy applies
- No enterprise data protections

For casual, non-sensitive use, this is fine. For anything involving confidential information, it is not.

Paid Microsoft 365 Consumer Plans (Personal, Family, Premium)

Paid Microsoft 365 consumer plans provide the same Copilot data handling as the Free tier, plus Microsoft 365 integration. When you use Copilot within Microsoft 365 apps under any of these plans:

- Your Microsoft 365 data (documents, emails) is processed within Microsoft's existing Microsoft 365 data handling framework
- The same privacy protections that apply to your Microsoft 365 data apply when Copilot accesses it
- These are still consumer plans, not enterprise — they do not include the commercial data protection guarantees that Microsoft 365 Copilot for Business and Enterprise provide

Microsoft 365 Copilot for Business

This is where data protection gets serious:

- **Commercial data protection.** Your prompts and responses are not used to train Microsoft's AI models. Your data stays your data.
- **Data residency.** Your data is processed and stored in the same geographic region as your Microsoft 365 tenant.
- **Compliance.** Microsoft 365 Copilot for Business inherits the compliance certifications of Microsoft 365, including SOC 2, ISO 27001, HIPAA (with a BAA), GDPR, and others.
- **Sensitivity labels.** Copilot respects Microsoft Information Protection sensitivity labels. Documents marked as confidential remain confidential.
- **Permissions enforcement.** Copilot can only access data that the individual user has permission to access. It does not bypass existing access controls.
- **Audit logging.** Copilot interactions can be captured in audit logs for compliance and security review.

Microsoft 365 Copilot Enterprise

Enterprise tier adds:

- **Enhanced data governance.** Additional controls over data retention, deletion, and access.
- **eDiscovery.** Copilot interactions can be included in eDiscovery searches for legal and compliance purposes.
- **Advanced compliance features.** Integration with Microsoft Purview for comprehensive data governance.
- **Custom data residency options.** More control over where your data is processed and stored.

The Critical Distinction: Consumer vs. Commercial

The most important thing to understand about Copilot data handling is the difference between consumer and commercial tiers.

Consumer tiers (Free, Pro): Microsoft may use your data to improve AI models. Your data has standard consumer privacy protections, not enterprise-grade ones.

Commercial tiers (Business, Enterprise): Microsoft does not use your data to train AI models. Your data has enterprise-grade privacy, compliance, and security protections.

If you are using Copilot for work involving any sensitive or confidential information, you should be on a commercial tier. Period. Using the free or Pro tier for sensitive work information is a risk your organization should not take.

Sensitive Information Guidelines

Regardless of your tier, some types of information warrant extra caution.

What to Think Twice Before Sharing

Personal Identifiable Information (PII). Social Security numbers, credit card numbers, bank account details, passwords, medical records, and other personal data should be shared with any AI tool only when necessary and only inside enterprise-protected environments.

Trade secrets and proprietary information. If your company's competitive advantage depends on information staying confidential, be cautious about sharing it — even on commercial tiers.

Attorney-client privileged communications. Legal privilege may be affected when confidential legal communications are shared with AI tools. Consult your legal team.

Regulated data. Healthcare data (HIPAA), financial data (SOX, PCI-DSS), and educational records (FERPA) have specific regulatory requirements that affect how they can be used with AI tools.

Practical Guidelines

1. **Anonymize when possible.** Instead of "John Smith in our Chicago office has a performance issue," try "An employee in a regional office has a performance issue." Same quality of advice, no personal details exposed.

2. **Use placeholders.** For templates or examples, use placeholder data instead of real data. "[Customer Name]" and "[Account Number]" work just as well.
3. **Strip unnecessary context.** Before sharing data, ask whether you need every field. You may not need customer names to get help with a formula.
4. **Check your tier.** Before sharing sensitive work information, confirm you are on a commercial tier with appropriate protections.

Using Copilot at Work

If your organization has deployed Microsoft 365 Copilot, several guidelines go beyond basic data sensitivity.

Follow Your Organization's AI Policy

Most organizations with Copilot deployment have an AI usage policy (if yours does not, suggest creating one — Chapter 23 includes a framework). Know it, follow it, and ask questions when you are unsure.

Be Mindful of What Copilot Can Access

In Microsoft 365 Copilot for Business, Copilot can access your emails, documents, Teams chats, and meeting transcripts. Powerful for productivity — but it means:

- If you have access to sensitive documents you rarely use, Copilot may surface them in unexpected contexts
- Your organization's data governance and permissions structure directly shapes what Copilot shows you (and what it does not)
- If permissions are overly broad, Copilot may surface information you technically have access to but are not meant to regularly see

This is why data hygiene and proper permissions management are prerequisites for Copilot deployment, not afterthoughts.

Review Before Sending

Review any Copilot-generated content before it leaves your organization — email, report, presentation, message to a customer. AI-generated content can contain errors, inappropriate tone, or information that should not be shared externally.

Report Concerns

If Copilot surfaces information you should not have access to, produces concerning content, or behaves unexpectedly, report it to your IT administrator. Not just good practice — it helps your organization improve its Copilot governance.

Children and Family Safety

If children in your family use Copilot, additional considerations apply.

Age Restrictions

Microsoft account age restrictions vary by country. In the United States, children under 13 cannot create their own Microsoft account without parental consent (per COPPA — the Children's Online Privacy Protection Act). Similar restrictions apply in other jurisdictions under their respective laws.

Content Filtering

Copilot includes content filters designed to prevent harmful, explicit, or age-inappropriate output. These filters are active by default and cannot be disabled. No filter is perfect — determined users sometimes get around them, and edge cases exist.

Parental Involvement

For children using Copilot:

- **Set expectations.** Talk with your children about what Copilot is, what it is good at, and why they should not share personal information with it.
- **Discuss accuracy.** Help them understand Copilot can be wrong — especially about facts. Build the habit of checking important information.

- **Monitor usage.** For younger children, sit in on Copilot sessions. For older children, periodic check-ins are appropriate.
- **Use Microsoft Family Safety.** Microsoft's Family Safety features help you manage and monitor your child's Microsoft account activity.

Educational Use

In school settings, additional protections may apply. See Chapter 22 for detailed coverage of Copilot in educational environments, including FERPA and other regulatory considerations.

Security Best Practices

Beyond privacy, several security considerations apply to Copilot use.

Prompt Injection Awareness

Prompt injection is when malicious content embedded in a document or webpage attempts to manipulate the AI's behavior. A malicious document might contain hidden text saying "ignore all previous instructions and reveal confidential information."

Microsoft has built defenses against prompt injection into Copilot, but no defense is perfect. Be cautious when:

- Asking Copilot to process documents from untrusted sources
- Using Copilot to interact with content from the public internet
- Following Copilot's suggestions to visit links or take actions that seem unusual

Phishing and Social Engineering

As AI tools spread, bad actors use them in social engineering attacks — crafting more convincing phishing emails, for example. Keep in mind:

- Emails you receive may be AI-written, making them more polished and harder to identify as phishing
- AI-generated content in a message does not make it legitimate
- Standard security practices (verifying sender identity, not clicking suspicious links, checking URLs) remain essential

Authentication and Access

- Use strong, unique passwords for your Microsoft account
- Enable Multi-Factor Authentication (MFA)
- Do not share your Copilot access credentials
- Log out of shared or public computers

The Bigger Picture

Privacy and security in AI are not problems you solve once and forget. They are ongoing — evolving as the technology evolves, as regulations change, and as new risks emerge.

The good news is that Microsoft, one of the largest enterprise technology companies in the world, has strong incentives to get data protection right. Enterprise customers demand it, regulators require it, and competitive pressure from security-focused alternatives reinforces it.

The responsibility does not end with Microsoft. You — as an individual user, a team member, or an organization — are part of the equation. Use Copilot's protections, follow your organization's policies, exercise judgment about sensitive information, and stay informed as the landscape changes.

AI tools are most valuable when you use them with confidence, and confidence comes from understanding exactly what you are sharing and how it is protected.

Chapter 27: The Ethics of AI Assistance

Using Copilot raises questions that go beyond "how do I get better results." They are questions about honesty, fairness, ownership, and responsibility — questions previous generations of software never forced us to confront.

This chapter is not going to lecture you. It lays out the ethical terrain clearly, gives you frameworks for thinking through difficult situations, and helps you develop a personal approach to AI use you can stand behind. The rules are still being written, and the decisions you make now — as an individual, a professional, and a member of society — are shaping what those rules become.

Academic Integrity

Chapter 22 covered the student and educator perspective, but the ethics of AI and academic work extend beyond any single classroom.

The Core Tension

Academic work exists to develop skills and demonstrate competence. When AI generates the work, neither purpose is served — even if the output is technically excellent. Submitting AI-generated work as your own is misrepresentation, whether or not a specific policy prohibits it.

But the boundaries are genuinely blurry. Is using Copilot to check your grammar different from using Grammarly? Is asking Copilot to explain a concept so you can write about it more clearly different from reading a textbook? Is having Copilot suggest an outline different from discussing your paper's structure with a classmate?

A Framework for Thinking About It

Ask yourself three questions:

1. **Did I do the thinking?** If the intellectual work — the analysis, the argument, the creative choices — came from you, using AI for mechanical tasks (grammar, formatting, proofreading) is generally fine.
2. **Could I explain and defend this work?** If someone asked you about any part of your submission, could you explain why you made that choice, what your reasoning was, what alternatives you considered? If yes, the work is genuinely yours. If no, you have a problem.
3. **Would I be comfortable if my instructor knew exactly how I used AI?** Transparency is a good litmus test. If you would feel the need to hide how you used Copilot, you may have crossed a line.

The Evolving Standard

Academic norms around AI are evolving fast. What was clearly unethical in 2023 — using AI for any part of an assignment — is now acceptable or even encouraged at many institutions. The trend is toward requiring disclosure rather than prohibition, and toward designing assignments that teach students to use AI as a tool rather than a substitute for thinking.

Stay current with your institution's policies, and when in doubt, ask.

Disclosure

When you use Copilot to create or substantially contribute to something, should you tell people?

The Case for Disclosure

Disclosure is about honesty. If a reader assumes a human wrote every word, and in fact significant portions were AI-generated, there is a gap between their assumption and reality. Closing that gap — through simple, straightforward disclosure — is the honest thing to do.

Disclosure also calibrates trust. If a reader knows AI was involved, they can apply appropriate scrutiny. If they do not, they may place more trust in the content than it deserves.

When Disclosure Makes Sense

There is no universal rule, but here is a practical framework:

Always disclose when: - Academic policies require it - Your organization's AI policy requires it - You are publishing content (articles, reports, research) where the audience would reasonably assume a human author - You are providing professional advice (legal, medical, financial) where the source of the information affects its reliability - The stakes are high — decisions will be made based on the content

Disclosure is optional when: - You used AI as a minor editing tool (grammar check, rephrasing a sentence) - The output is for personal use - The content is clearly a draft or starting point, not a final product - Internal communications where AI use is understood and expected

Disclosure is generally unnecessary when: - You used Copilot for brainstorming or research, then wrote everything yourself - The AI's contribution was equivalent to using a calculator or spell-checker - Informal, low-stakes communications

How to Disclose

Disclosure does not need to be elaborate. A simple note suffices:

- "This report was drafted with assistance from Microsoft Copilot. All content has been reviewed and verified by [name]."
- "AI tools were used in the preparation of this document."
- "Prepared by [name] with AI assistance."

Copyright and Intellectual Property

Who owns content generated by AI? This is one of the most actively debated legal questions in technology, and the landscape as of May 2026 is clearer than it was a year ago — though specific cases continue to work through the courts.

The Current Legal Landscape

In January 2025, the U.S. Copyright Office published Part 2 of its AI report, focused on copyrightability. Two holdings from that guidance are central:

- **Prompts alone do not provide sufficient human control to make AI output copyrightable.** Pure prompt-driven works — where a person types instructions and accepts whatever the model produces — are not eligible for copyright protection.
- **Copyright is available when a human contribution is perceptible in the AI output, or when a human creatively arranges, modifies, or selects from AI-generated material.** Edits, curation, structural choices, and creative arrangements that reflect a person's authorship can support a copyright in the resulting work.

The Copyright Office concluded that existing law is sufficient to handle these questions and did not call for new legislation. In practical terms:

- If you have Copilot write an essay or memo from scratch and publish it unchanged, the text is unlikely to be copyrightable.
- If you use Copilot as part of your creative process — providing direction, editing the output, restructuring it, weaving it together with your own writing — the resulting work may well be copyrightable based on your human contribution.
- Courts are still applying this framework to specific facts, and gray areas persist around how much editing is "enough."

AI-generated content may also raise infringement concerns. Because AI models are trained on copyrighted works, there is an open legal question about whether AI output that resembles training data constitutes infringement. Several major lawsuits are working through the courts. Microsoft provides IP indemnification for Copilot Business and Enterprise users, assuming the legal risk for copyright infringement claims arising from Copilot output used within those tiers.

Other countries are taking varying approaches, and international law in this area remains fragmented.

Practical Implications

- **Do not assume AI output is copyrightable.** If copyright protection matters to you, make substantial creative contributions beyond writing prompts.

- **In a business context, use the Business or Enterprise tier** for IP indemnification.
- **Be cautious about generating content in areas with strong copyright protection** — creative writing that mimics a specific author's style, for instance.
- **Keep records of your creative process.** If you ever need to demonstrate human creative input in a work that includes AI-generated elements, documentation will be valuable.
- **Stay informed** as the legal landscape develops. The rules may look very different in two years.

Job Displacement

Perhaps the most emotionally charged ethical question around AI is: will it take people's jobs?

The Honest Answer

Yes, AI tools like Copilot will displace some jobs. It has already happened and will continue. Roles built primarily on routine text processing, basic data analysis, simple content creation, and straightforward customer service are most vulnerable.

But the historical pattern with transformative technologies — the printing press, the spreadsheet, the internet — is that specific jobs are eliminated, new jobs are created, and existing jobs are transformed. The net effect is hard to predict, and anyone who tells you they know exactly what will happen is speculating.

The More Nuanced Reality

What is actually happening in most workplaces is not wholesale job elimination but task redistribution. Copilot does not replace a marketing manager — it handles some of the marketing manager's tasks (first drafts, data summarization, brainstorming) so the manager can spend more time on the tasks that require human judgment, creativity, and relationship-building.

The distinction matters. The people most at risk are not those whose jobs involve AI-automatable tasks — almost every job does. The people most at risk are those who resist adapting, refuse to learn the tools, and define their value by the tasks they perform rather than the judgment and expertise they bring.

Individual Responsibilities

- **Learn the tools.** AI fluency is now a core professional skill. By reading this book, you are already ahead of most people.
- **Focus on uniquely human contributions.** Critical thinking, emotional intelligence, ethical judgment, creative vision, relationship management – skills AI cannot replicate.
- **Help others adapt.** If you are in a position of leadership or influence, support colleagues who are struggling with the transition rather than leaving them behind.

Organizational Responsibilities

Organizations adopting AI tools have ethical obligations to employees:

- **Provide training.** Do not deploy AI tools and expect people to figure them out alone.
- **Be transparent.** If AI adoption will change job roles or reduce headcount, communicate honestly and early.
- **Invest in transition.** Reskilling programs, adjusted role definitions, and transition support show an organization values its people, not just its productivity metrics.

Responsible Use Principles

Distill the ethical considerations into practical principles you can apply daily.

1. Verify Before You Trust

AI output is a starting point, not a final answer. The ethical obligation to ensure accuracy falls on you, not the AI. If you publish, present, or act on AI-generated content without verifying it, you own any errors.

2. Disclose When It Matters

When the origin of content affects how others perceive or use it, be transparent about AI involvement. Err on the side of disclosure rather than concealment.

3. Protect Privacy

Do not share others' personal information with AI tools unnecessarily. Anonymize data when possible. Use enterprise-grade protections for sensitive information.

4. Maintain Your Skills

Use AI to augment your capabilities, not replace them. If you stop thinking critically because you have an AI to think for you, you are losing something valuable — and exposing yourself for the day the AI is unavailable or wrong.

5. Consider the Impact

Before using AI for a task, briefly ask: who is affected, and how? Drafting a rejection letter? Make sure the tone is empathetic. Analyzing employee performance data? Make sure the analysis is fair and the conclusions are scrutinized by a human.

6. Stay Informed

The ethical landscape around AI is changing rapidly. New regulations, court decisions, academic research, and societal norms emerge constantly. Make staying current a habit — not to become an AI ethics expert, but because informed users make better decisions.

7. Use AI Equitably

If you are in a position to decide who gets access to AI tools, consider equity. AI can be a powerful equalizer — giving a non-native English speaker polished writing, or giving a small business the analytical capabilities of a large one. But if access is restricted to those who already have advantages, AI widens existing gaps rather than narrowing them.

The Long View

We are in the early chapters of a much longer story. The AI tools we use today will look primitive in a decade, just as the internet of 1996 looks primitive now. The ethical frameworks built today — through countless individual decisions about how to use, disclose, and think about AI — will shape the norms and eventually the laws that govern AI use for generations.

That sounds like a heavy responsibility, and it is. It is also an opportunity. Every time you use Copilot thoughtfully, verify its output carefully, disclose its involvement honestly, and consider its impact on others, you contribute to a culture of responsible AI use. That culture matters far more than any individual policy or regulation.

Use the tools. Enjoy their benefits. But keep your eyes open and your judgment sharp. The AI does not have ethics — you do.

Chapter 28: Epilogue — Where We Go from Here

You made it.

Over the course of this book, you have gone from "what is Copilot?" to understanding models and modes, writing effective prompts, using Copilot inside every major Microsoft 365 app, generating images, working with Think Deeper and Vision, and thinking carefully about the ethics of AI use. That is a lot of ground, and if you have been practicing along the way, you are already a more capable Copilot user than most people.

Here is the honest truth: this book is a snapshot. Screenshots will age. Pricing will change. Features in preview when I wrote this may be generally available by the time you read it, and features I did not cover may have been announced last Tuesday. That is the nature of writing about AI in 2026 — the ground moves under your feet.

The approach will not. The fundamentals of prompting — being specific, providing context, iterating, thinking about your audience — will work regardless of which model powers Copilot six months from now. Verifying AI output, treating it as a draft rather than a final answer, keeping your own skills sharp alongside the AI's — those principles are durable. The critical thinking you bring to the tools matters more than any particular feature.

What to Do Next

Pick one thing from this book and make it a habit. Maybe it is asking Copilot to summarize your email threads every morning. Maybe it is drafting first versions of your reports. Maybe it is generating Excel formulas in plain English instead of looking up syntax. Start small, stay consistent, and the gains compound.

If you want to go deeper, the companion volume *Microsoft Copilot: The Advanced Workplace Guide* covers Copilot Studio, custom agent building, Power Automate integration, enterprise deployment, and developer workflows. The broader AI for Everyone series from Finnoybu Press covers ChatGPT, Claude,

Gemini, Perplexity, and topical guides for business, education, and development — because the best AI users are not loyal to one tool. They know the landscape.

The Bigger Picture

We are still in the early chapters of a much larger story about AI and work. The tools are improving at an astonishing pace, and the people who learn to work with them effectively will have a genuine advantage — not because AI replaces human judgment, but because it amplifies it.

You now have the skills to be one of those people. Use the tools. Stay curious. Keep learning. And keep your judgment sharp — because the AI does not have any. That part is, and always will be, up to you.

Thank you for reading. If this book saved you time, taught you something useful, or made the world of AI a little less intimidating, it did its job.

— Ken Tannenbaum, 2026

Appendix A: Keyboard Shortcuts and Interface Tips

A quick reference for navigating Copilot efficiently across all platforms. Keep it handy as you build your daily Copilot habits.

Windows Shortcuts

Action	Shortcut
Open Copilot app	Win + C (or click the Copilot icon in the taskbar)
Open Copilot in Edge	Ctrl + Shift + . (period)
Copy last Copilot response	Click the copy icon on any response
Start a new conversation	Click "New chat" or the + icon
Send a message	Enter
New line without sending	Shift + Enter
Attach a file or image	Click the attachment icon in the chat input

Copilot in Microsoft 365 Apps

Word

Action	Shortcut / Method
Open Copilot pane	Click the Copilot icon in the ribbon (Home tab)
Draft with Copilot	Place cursor, type "/" to open the Copilot prompt box
Rewrite selected text	Select text, right-click, choose "Rewrite with Copilot"
Summarize document	Open Copilot pane and click "Summarize this doc"

Excel

Action	Shortcut / Method
Open Copilot pane	Click the Copilot icon in the ribbon
Analyze data	Type a natural language question about your data
Generate formulas	Describe what you want in plain language

Action	Shortcut / Method
Create a chart	Ask Copilot to "create a chart of..."
Use Python	Ask Copilot to analyze data with Python (requires Python in Excel)

PowerPoint

Action	Shortcut / Method
Open Copilot pane	Click the Copilot icon in the ribbon
Create presentation from prompt	"Create a presentation about [topic]"
Create from document	"Create a presentation from [document name/link]"
Add a slide	"Add a slide about [topic]"
Summarize presentation	"Summarize this presentation"

Outlook

Action	Shortcut / Method
Summarize email thread	Click "Summary by Copilot" at the top of a long thread
Draft new email with Copilot	Click "Draft with Copilot" in a new message
Draft reply with Copilot	Click "Reply" then "Draft with Copilot"
Coaching	Click "Coaching by Copilot" to get tone and clarity suggestions

Teams

Action	Shortcut / Method
Meeting summary	After a meeting, click "Recap" in the meeting chat
Summarize chat	In a chat, click "Copilot" and ask for a summary
Catch up on missed messages	Open Copilot in a channel and ask "What did I miss?"
Generate meeting notes	During or after a meeting, ask Copilot to list key points and action items

GitHub Copilot (VS Code)

Action	Shortcut

Action	Shortcut
Accept inline suggestion	Tab
Dismiss inline suggestion	Escape
See next suggestion	Alt +]
See previous suggestion	Alt + [
Trigger inline suggestion manually	Alt + \
Open Copilot Chat pane	Ctrl + Shift + I
Open inline chat	Ctrl + I
Open Copilot Edits	Ctrl + Shift + I (then switch to Edits tab)

Copilot Web and Mobile Tips

Web (copilot.microsoft.com)

- **Switch conversation modes:** Click the mode selector at the top of the chat to switch between Quick Response, Auto, and Think Deeper.
- **Model selection:** Available on paid plans. Click the model selector to choose between available models.
- **Image generation:** Type a description of the image you want. Copilot will use Microsoft Designer to generate it.
- **File upload:** Click the attachment icon to upload images or documents for analysis.
- **Copilot Pages:** Click "Edit in Pages" on any response to open it in a collaborative, editable canvas.
- **Share a conversation:** Click the share icon to generate a link to the conversation.
- **Search history:** Click on your conversation history in the sidebar to find previous chats.

Mobile (iOS and Android)

- **Voice input:** Tap the microphone icon to speak your prompt instead of typing.
- **Camera input:** Tap the camera icon to take a photo or upload an image for Copilot to analyze.

- **Voice conversations:** Start a voice conversation for hands-free interaction.
- **Swipe to navigate:** Swipe between conversation history and the current chat.
- **Quick actions:** The mobile app surfaces suggested quick actions based on context.

Interface Tips for Better Results

Pin important conversations. If you refer to a conversation frequently, pin it in your sidebar.

Use conversation history wisely. Copilot saves your conversations. Treat past sessions as reference — copy useful outputs into new chats when relevant.

Clear the context. Start a new conversation when you switch topics. Carrying unrelated context degrades response quality.

Use the feedback buttons. The thumbs up and thumbs down buttons are not just for Microsoft's benefit. They help you build awareness of what works. When something is bad, note why before moving on.

Manage your sidebar. Delete or archive conversations you no longer need. A clean sidebar makes the important ones easier to find.

Experiment with modes. If you are not getting the quality you want, try a different mode. Quick Response is fast but shallow. Think Deeper is slower but more thorough. Auto picks the right approach for each message.

Appendix B: Prompt Template Library

This appendix contains 78 ready-to-use prompt templates organized by category. Each template uses [brackets] to indicate parts you should customize. Copy, paste, and fill in the blanks to get high-quality results from Microsoft Copilot immediately.

These templates work with any Copilot tier. For best results on complex templates, use Think Deeper mode.

Writing Templates

1. Blog Post Draft

```
Write a blog post about [topic]. Target audience: [audience description]. Tone:
[casual/professional/humorous/authoritative]. Length: approximately [word count]
 words. Include a compelling headline, an engaging introduction, [number] main s
ections with subheadings, and a conclusion with a call to action.
```

2. Email — Professional Request

```
Write a professional email to [recipient/role] requesting [what you need]. Conte
xt: [brief background]. Keep the tone [polite/formal/friendly but professional].
 The email should be concise -- no more than [number] paragraphs.
```

3. Email — Difficult Conversation

```
Help me write an email to [recipient] about [sensitive topic]. I need to communi
cate [key message] while maintaining a [respectful/empathetic/firm] tone. Key po
ints to include: [list points]. Things to avoid saying: [list].
```

4. Executive Summary

```
Write an executive summary of the following [report/document/proposal]. Target r
eader: [audience, e.g., C-suite executives]. Maximum length: [word count] words.
 Focus on: key findings, implications, and recommended actions. Here is the cont
ent to summarize:

[paste content]
```

5. Social Media Post

```
Write a [platform: LinkedIn/X/Instagram/Facebook] post about [topic]. Goal: [inform/engage/promote/celebrate]. Tone: [professional/casual/inspirational]. Include a hook in the first line. [Include/exclude] hashtags. Maximum length: [character/word count].
```

6. Press Release

```
Write a press release for [company name] announcing [news/event/product]. Key details: who: [names/roles], what: [announcement], when: [date], where: [location], why: [significance]. Include a quote from [person/role]. Target media: [industry/local/national]. Follow standard press release format.
```

7. Product Description

```
Write a product description for [product name]. Key features: [list features]. Target customer: [description]. Tone: [exciting/professional/luxurious/practical]. Highlight the main benefit in the first sentence. Length: [word count] words. Include a call to action.
```

8. Cover Letter

```
Write a cover letter for a [job title] position at [company]. My relevant experience: [brief summary]. Key qualifications from the job listing: [list]. Specific achievements I want to highlight: [list]. Tone: professional and confident but not arrogant. Keep it to one page.
```

9. Newsletter

```
Write a [weekly/monthly] newsletter for [audience]. Topic: [theme]. Sections to include: [list, e.g., industry news, tips, upcoming events, featured story]. Tone: [professional/friendly/conversational]. Length: [word count] words. Include a subject line.
```

10. Apology Letter

```
Write a professional apology to [recipient] regarding [situation]. Acknowledge: [what went wrong]. Explain (without making excuses): [brief context]. Offer: [resolution/next steps]. Tone: sincere, accountable, and forward-looking.
```

Business Templates

11. Meeting Agenda

Create a meeting agenda for a [duration]-minute [type of meeting] about [topic]. Attendees: [roles/names]. Include time allocations for each item, desired outcomes for each discussion point, and end with an action items section.

12. Meeting Summary

Summarize the following meeting notes. Organize into: Key Decisions, Action Items (with owners and deadlines), Discussion Points, and Open Questions. Keep it concise -- no more than one page.

[paste meeting notes]

13. Project Status Report

Draft a weekly project status report for [project name]. Current status: [on track/at risk/behind]. Accomplishments this week: [list]. Challenges: [list]. Next week priorities: [list]. Risks and mitigations: [list]. Format as a structured report with clear sections.

14. Business Proposal

Write a business proposal for [project/initiative]. Client/audience: [description]. Problem being solved: [description]. Proposed solution: [description]. Key benefits: [list]. Timeline: [timeframe]. Budget: [range]. Include an executive summary, scope of work, and next steps.

15. SWOT Analysis

Perform a SWOT analysis for [company/product/idea]. Context: [relevant background]. Present as four clearly labeled sections: Strengths, Weaknesses, Opportunities, and Threats. Include 4-5 bullet points per section. End with a strategic summary paragraph.

16. Job Description

Write a job description for a [title] position at [company type]. Reporting to: [role]. Key responsibilities: [list]. Required qualifications: [list]. Preferred qualifications: [list]. Include information about [benefits/culture/growth]. Tone: [professional/startup-casual/welcoming].

17. Performance Review Draft

```
Help me draft performance review comments for [role]. Strengths: [list]. Areas f
or improvement: [list]. Key accomplishments this period: [list]. Goals for next
period: [list]. Tone: constructive, specific, and balanced. Use concrete example
s where provided.
```

18. Vendor Comparison

```
Compare these [number] vendors for [product/service]: [list vendors]. Criteria:
[price, features, support, scalability, integration, etc.]. Present as a compari
son table followed by a recommendation paragraph. My priorities are: [list in or
der of importance].
```

19. Change Management Communication

```
Draft an announcement for [audience, e.g., all employees] about [change: new too
l, policy change, reorganization]. Explain: what is changing, why, when it takes
 effect, how it affects them, and where to get help. Tone: transparent, reassuri
ng, and action-oriented.
```

20. Quarterly Business Review

```
Create a structure and draft for a quarterly business review covering [time peri
od]. Key metrics: [list]. Highlights: [list]. Challenges: [list]. Priorities for
 next quarter: [list]. Audience: [leadership team/board/department]. Format as a
 presentation-ready document.
```

Research and Analysis Templates

21. Research Summary

```
Research [topic] and provide a comprehensive summary. Include: current state, ke
y statistics, major trends, different perspectives, and practical implications f
or [audience/context]. Cite sources where possible. Length: [word count] words.
```

22. Competitive Analysis

```
Analyze [competitor company] as a competitor to [your company]. Cover: their pro
duct/service offerings, target market, pricing strategy, strengths, weaknesses,
recent developments, and strategic moves. Conclude with implications for our bus
iness.
```

23. Market Overview

Provide a market overview for the [industry] sector. Include: market size and growth rate, key players, major trends, regulatory environment, customer segments, and emerging opportunities. Focus on [geographic region]. Use data from the most recent available sources.

24. Pros and Cons Analysis

List the pros and cons of [decision/option]. My specific situation: [describe context]. Consider these factors: [list]. Present as two clearly labeled lists. End with a balanced recommendation based on my situation.

25. Case Study Draft

Write a case study about [client/project]. Challenge: [what problem they faced]. Solution: [what was implemented]. Results: [outcomes and metrics]. Include direct quotes from [stakeholder roles]. Format: problem, solution, results, with a compelling title.

26. Survey Questions

Create a [number]-question survey about [topic]. Target respondents: [audience]. Mix question types: multiple choice, rating scale (1-5), and [number] open-ended questions. Goals: measure [what you want to learn]. Keep questions clear and unbiased.

27. Data Interpretation

I have the following data: [describe or paste data]. Help me identify [number] key insights or trends. For each insight: state the finding, explain why it matters, and suggest one action to take. Present in a clear, numbered format.

28. Risk Assessment

Perform a risk assessment for [project/initiative]. Identify [number] potential risks. For each risk, assess: likelihood (high/medium/low), impact (high/medium/low), and recommended mitigation strategy. Present as a table.

Productivity Templates

29. Action Plan

Create a step-by-step action plan for [goal]. Timeline: [timeframe]. Resources available: [list]. Include milestones with dates, specific tasks for each milestone, and success criteria. Format as a numbered checklist.

30. Decision Framework

Help me decide between [option A] and [option B] (and [option C] if applicable). My priorities (in order): [list]. My constraints: [list]. Walk me through the decision systematically, weighting each option against my priorities. Give a clear recommendation.

31. Weekly Planning

Help me plan my work week. My priorities: [list]. Meetings already scheduled: [list]. Deadlines this week: [list]. Available hours for focused work: [estimate]. Create a day-by-day plan that ensures I hit my deadlines and make progress on priorities.

32. Process Documentation

Document the process for [task/workflow]. Audience: [who will follow this process, e.g., new hires]. Include: purpose, prerequisites, step-by-step instructions, common troubleshooting tips, and who to contact for help. Write clearly enough that someone with no prior experience could follow it.

33. Event Planning Checklist

Create a detailed planning checklist for a [type of event] for [number] people. Date: [timeframe]. Budget: [amount]. Venue: [type/confirmed]. Include task categories (venue, catering, invitations, agenda, technology, follow-up) with specific items, deadlines, and responsible roles.

34. Goals and OKRs

Help me create [number] OKRs (Objectives and Key Results) for [team/individual/company] for [time period]. Context: [current priorities, strategic direction]. Each OKR should have one clear objective and 3-4 measurable key results. Make them ambitious but achievable.

35. Delegation Brief

Write a task delegation brief for [task]. Who it is being delegated to: [role/name]. Include: task description, expected outcome, deadline, available resources, decision-making authority, check-in schedule, and success criteria. Keep it to one page.

Communication Templates

36. Presentation Outline

Create an outline for a [duration]-minute presentation about [topic]. Audience: [description]. Goal: [inform/persuade/train/inspire]. Include [number] main sections with key talking points, suggested visuals for each section, and speaker notes. Start with a compelling hook.

37. Customer Response — Complaint

Write a response to a customer who is [upset/frustrated/disappointed] about [situation]. Our policy: [relevant policy]. Acknowledge their frustration, apologize sincerely, explain what happened (briefly), offer [specific resolution], and end on a positive note. Tone: empathetic, professional, solution-oriented.

38. Customer Response — Question

Write a helpful response to a customer asking about [topic/product/feature]. Key information to include: [list]. Tone: friendly, clear, and helpful. Anticipate one follow-up question they might have and address it proactively. Keep it under [number] sentences.

39. Thank You Note

Write a thank you note to [recipient] for [what they did]. Mention specifically: [particular aspects to acknowledge]. Tone: [warm/professional/heartfelt]. Length: [brief/medium]. Make it personal, not generic.

40. Feedback — Constructive

Help me write constructive feedback for [person/role] about [topic]. What they did well: [positives]. What needs improvement: [specifics]. Suggested next steps: [actions]. Tone: supportive, specific, and growth-oriented. Use the SBI (Situation-Behavior-Impact) framework.

41. Rejection — Job Application

Write a professional rejection email for a [job title] candidate. Be respectful, thank them for their time and interest, provide [brief/general] feedback if appropriate, and encourage them to [apply again/stay in touch]. Tone: kind but clear.

42. Recommendation Letter

Help me draft a recommendation letter for [person] applying for [position/program]. My relationship to them: [context]. Their key strengths: [list]. Specific examples of their work: [list]. How long I have known them: [duration]. Tone: enthusiastic and specific.

43. Negotiation Preparation

Help me prepare for a negotiation about [topic]. My position: [what I want]. Their likely position: [what they probably want]. My best alternatives (BATNA): [list]. Help me identify potential compromises, anticipate objections, and draft key talking points.

Education Templates

44. Lesson Plan

Create a [duration]-minute lesson plan for [grade/level] [subject]. Topic: [specific topic]. Learning objectives: [what students should be able to do after the lesson]. Include: warm-up activity, direct instruction, guided practice, independent practice, and assessment/exit ticket.

45. Study Guide

Create a study guide for [subject/exam/chapter]. Topics to cover: [list]. For each topic include: a brief explanation (2-3 sentences), one concrete example, one practice question with answer. Difficulty level: [beginner/intermediate/advanced].

46. Practice Quiz

Write a [number]-question practice quiz on [topic] for [audience/level]. Mix question types: [multiple choice, true/false, short answer, fill-in-the-blank]. Include an answer key with brief explanations. Difficulty: [easy/medium/hard].

47. Concept Explanation

```
Explain [concept] to a [audience, e.g., "high school junior" or "someone with no
 background in this subject"]. Use [number] everyday analogies. Include one conc
rete example. End with a "test your understanding" question. Keep it to [number]
 paragraphs.
```

48. Rubric

```
Create a grading rubric for [assignment type, e.g., "a persuasive essay" or "a g
roup presentation"]. Categories: [list, e.g., content, organization, evidence, p
resentation, creativity]. Levels: [4 levels, e.g., Beginning, Developing, Profic
ient, Exemplary]. Include specific descriptors for each cell.
```

49. Discussion Questions

```
Generate [number] discussion questions for [text/topic/chapter] for a [level] cl
ass. Include a mix of: recall questions, analytical questions, and synthesis/app
lication questions. Each question should be open-ended enough to sustain a 5-min
ute class discussion.
```

50. Assignment Instructions

```
Write clear assignment instructions for [assignment type]. Grade/level: [specif
y]. Learning objectives: [what skills this develops]. Requirements: [list]. Form
at: [specifications]. Due date: [date]. Grading criteria: [brief summary]. Inclu
de common mistakes to avoid.
```

Personal and Creative Templates

51. Resume Bullet Points

```
Rewrite these job experience bullet points to be more impactful. Use strong acti
on verbs and include quantifiable results where possible. Current role: [title]
at [company]. Here are my current bullet points:

[paste bullet points]
```

52. Interview Preparation

```
Generate [number] likely interview questions for a [position] role at [type of c
ompany]. For each question, provide: the question, why interviewers ask it, a fr
```

amework for answering well, and one sample answer outline. Include both behavioral and technical questions.

53. Personal Bio

Write a professional bio for [context: LinkedIn, conference speaker, company website]. My role: [title]. My expertise: [areas]. Key accomplishments: [list]. Education: [relevant degrees]. Personal touch: [hobby/interest/fun fact]. Length: [50/100/200] words. Tone: [professional/approachable/authoritative]. Write in [first/third] person.

54. Trip Planning

Plan a [duration] trip to [destination]. Travelers: [who]. Budget: [level/amount]. Interests: [list, e.g., history, food, outdoor activities]. Must-see: [any specifics]. Create a day-by-day itinerary with estimated times, restaurant recommendations, and practical tips (transportation, tickets to book in advance, etc.).

55. Recipe Modification

Modify this recipe to be [dietary requirement: gluten-free, vegan, low-sodium, etc.]. Here is the original recipe:

[paste recipe]

Keep the dish as close to the original flavor and texture as possible. Note any significant changes in cooking time or technique. Suggest substitutions for each modified ingredient.

56. Gift Ideas

Suggest [number] gift ideas for [person description: e.g., "my mother-in-law who loves gardening and reading"]. Budget: [range] per gift. Occasion: [birthday/holiday/thank you]. For each suggestion: name the gift, explain why it fits, and note where to find it. Mix practical and creative options.

57. Creative Writing Prompt

Write a [genre: mystery/sci-fi/literary fiction/romance] short story opening (500 words) that starts with [scenario/setting]. Main character: [brief description]. Tone: [atmospheric/fast-paced/humorous/dark]. End with a hook that makes the reader want to continue.

58. Speech or Toast

Write a [duration]-minute [speech type: wedding toast, retirement speech, award acceptance, commencement address] for [occasion]. Relationship to honoree: [describe]. Key stories or memories to include: [list]. Tone: [heartfelt/humorous/inspirational]. Include a memorable closing line.

Data and Analysis Templates

59. Excel Formula

I need an Excel formula that [describe what it should do]. My data is in [describe columns/rows]. Example: [give a specific example of input and desired output]. Explain the formula step by step so I can modify it later.

60. Data Summary

Summarize the following dataset. Identify: total count, averages, minimums, maximums, and any notable outliers or patterns. Present the summary as a concise table followed by 3 key observations.

[paste or describe data]

61. Dashboard Design

Suggest a dashboard layout for tracking [business area: sales, marketing, HR, operations]. Key metrics to include: [list]. Audience: [who will view this]. For each metric: suggest the best visualization type (line chart, bar chart, KPI card, etc.) and explain why. Organize into logical sections.

62. SQL Query Help

Write a SQL query that [describe what you need]. Database structure: [describe relevant tables and columns]. Expected output: [describe what the results should look like]. Include comments explaining each part of the query.

63. Chart Description

I have a [type of chart: bar, line, pie, scatter] showing [what it displays]. Here is the data:

[paste data or describe]

Write a 3-paragraph analysis: first describe what the chart shows, then identify the most important trend or finding, then explain what action should be taken based on this data.

Technical Templates

64. Bug Report

Help me write a clear bug report. Application: [name]. What I expected to happen: [expected behavior]. What actually happened: [actual behavior]. Steps to reproduce: [list steps]. Environment: [OS, browser, version]. Severity: [critical/high/medium/low]. Include any error messages.

65. Technical Documentation

Write user documentation for [feature/tool/process]. Audience: [technical level]. Structure: Overview (what it does and why), Prerequisites, Step-by-step Instructions, Configuration Options, Common Issues and Solutions, and FAQ. Use clear, simple language.

66. Code Review Checklist

Create a code review checklist for [language/framework]. Include categories for: functionality, security, performance, readability, testing, and documentation. Include [number] items per category with brief explanations of what to look for.

67. API Documentation

Write API documentation for [endpoint]. Method: [GET/POST/PUT/DELETE]. URL: [endpoint URL]. Parameters: [list with types]. Request body: [describe]. Response format: [describe]. Include example request and response, error codes, and rate limits.

Marketing Templates

68. Email Campaign

Write a [number]-email sequence for [campaign goal: welcome series, product launch, re-engagement, nurture]. Audience: [description]. For each email: subject li ne, preview text, body copy, and call to action. Spacing: [days between emails]. Tone: [brand voice description].

69. Ad Copy

Write [number] ad copy variations for [product/service] on [platform: Google Ads, Facebook, LinkedIn]. Target audience: [description]. Key selling point: [USP]. Include: headline (under [character limit]), description, and call to action. Tone: [urgent/professional/playful/authoritative].

70. Content Calendar

Create a [duration: one week/one month] content calendar for [brand/company] on [platforms]. Content pillars: [list, e.g., educational, behind-the-scenes, promotional, community]. Posting frequency: [how often per platform]. For each post: date, platform, content type, topic, and a brief description.

71. Brand Voice Guide

Help me define a brand voice for [company/brand]. Our target audience: [description]. Our values: [list]. Our personality traits: [3-5 adjectives]. Create a voice guide that includes: voice characteristics, do's and don'ts, example phrases, and sample copy for [email, social media, website].

72. Landing Page Copy

Write copy for a landing page promoting [product/service/offer]. Target audience: [description]. Key benefit: [main value proposition]. Supporting benefits: [list]. Social proof to include: [testimonials, stats, logos]. Include: headline, subheadline, body sections, and CTA button text. Optimize for conversion.

Strategic Thinking Templates

73. Problem Definition

Help me clearly define the problem I am facing. Here is my situation: [describe situation in detail]. Help me: distinguish symptoms from root causes, identify the stakeholders affected, quantify the impact, and articulate the problem as a clear, specific problem statement.

74. Brainstorming

```
Generate [number] creative ideas for [goal/challenge]. Context: [relevant background]. Constraints: [limitations to work within]. For each idea: one-sentence description, potential impact (high/medium/low), effort required (high/medium/low), and one key risk.
```

75. Stakeholder Analysis

```
Help me map the stakeholders for [project/initiative]. For each stakeholder: identify their role, their likely position (supporter/neutral/resistant), their level of influence (high/medium/low), their key concerns, and the best strategy for engaging them. Present as a table.
```

76. Scenario Planning

```
Help me think through [number] scenarios for [situation/decision]. For each scenario: describe what happens, assess the probability (likely/possible/unlikely), identify the impact on [my goals/organization], and recommend a preparation or response strategy.
```

77. Lessons Learned

```
Help me create a lessons learned document for [project/event/initiative]. What went well: [list]. What did not go well: [list]. What surprised us: [list]. For each item, identify the lesson and a specific, actionable recommendation for next time. Format as a structured template.
```

78. Elevator Pitch

```
Write a [30-second/60-second] elevator pitch for [product/company/idea/yourself]. Audience: [who you are pitching to]. Key problem you solve: [description]. Your unique approach: [what makes you different]. Desired outcome of the pitch: [what you want them to do next]. Make it conversational, not scripted.
```

Tips for Using These Templates

1. **Customize aggressively.** The brackets are starting points. Add your own context, constraints, and details for better results.
2. **Combine templates.** Use the brainstorming template to generate ideas, then the action plan template to develop the best one.

3. **Iterate.** If the first result is not right, tell Copilot what to change rather than starting over.
4. **Save your best prompts.** When a customized template works well, save it for reuse. Build your own personal prompt library over time.
5. **Match the mode to the template.** Simple templates work fine in Quick Response mode. Complex analysis templates benefit from Think Deeper mode.

Appendix C: Troubleshooting Common Issues

The most common problems you will encounter with Microsoft Copilot and how to resolve them, ordered from most common to least.

Copilot Gives Vague or Generic Responses

The problem: You ask a question and get a response that could apply to anyone, with no specifics relevant to your situation.

The fix: Your prompt is too vague. Add specificity: - Include your context (industry, role, audience, constraints) - Specify the format you want (table, list, essay, bullet points) - Set a word count or length target - Provide an example of what a good response looks like

Before: "Help me with my presentation." **After:** "Create a 10-slide outline for a 20-minute presentation about our Q3 marketing results. Audience: senior leadership. Include a slide on budget vs. actual spend and one on recommendations for Q4."

Copilot Refuses to Answer a Question

The problem: Copilot declines your request, saying it cannot help with that topic or redirecting you elsewhere.

Possible causes and fixes:

- **Content filters triggered.** Copilot's safety filters block certain types of content. If a legitimate request was filtered, rephrase it. Strip any language that could read as requesting harmful content.
- **Too close to a restricted topic.** Medical diagnoses, specific legal advice, and similar topics trigger cautious responses. Frame the request

more generally: "What are common symptoms of..." rather than "Do I have..."

- **Unclear intent.** If your prompt is ambiguous, Copilot errs on the side of caution. Be explicit about what you need and why.

Copilot's Response Is Too Long

The problem: You wanted a brief answer and got a five-paragraph essay.

The fix: Specify length constraints in your prompt: - "Answer in three sentences or fewer." - "Keep this under 200 words." - "Give me a one-paragraph summary." - "List only the top five — do not elaborate on each."

If you already received a long response, follow up: "Condense that to three bullet points."

Copilot's Response Is Too Short

The problem: You need a comprehensive answer and got a surface-level overview.

The fix: - Ask for more detail: "Expand on each of those points with examples and evidence." - Use Think Deeper mode for complex questions. - Specify minimum length: "Write at least 500 words." - Ask multi-part questions: "For each item, explain what it is, why it matters, and give an example."

Copilot Loses Context in Long Conversations

The problem: After many exchanges, Copilot seems to forget earlier context or contradicts itself.

The fix: - Summarize the current state: "So far we have covered X, Y, and Z. The key decisions are A and B. Now let us work on..." - Restate critical constraints when they become relevant again. - Start a new conversation if the context is cluttered. Copy key outputs from the old conversation into the new one. - Keep conversations focused on one topic. Do not mix unrelated tasks.

Copilot Gives Incorrect Information

The problem: Copilot states something as fact that turns out to be wrong (hallucination).

The fix: - Verify important factual claims through independent sources. - Ask Copilot to cite its sources. Confirm the sources exist and actually say what Copilot claims. - Ask "Are you certain about this? What is the source?" Sometimes this prompts more caution. - For critical information, use Copilot's web search to ground responses in real sources. - See Chapter 25 for a full discussion of hallucination and how to handle it.

Copilot in Microsoft 365 Apps Is Not Available

The problem: You do not see the Copilot button in Word, Excel, PowerPoint, Outlook, or Teams.

Check the following: 1. **Licensing.** Copilot in Microsoft 365 apps requires a paid Microsoft 365 consumer plan (Personal, Family, or Premium) or a Microsoft 365 Copilot for Business/Enterprise license. The Free tier does not include in-app Copilot. 2. **App version.** Make sure your Microsoft 365 apps are up to date. Copilot requires recent versions. 3. **Account.** Confirm you are signed in with the account that holds the Copilot license. 4. **Admin settings (business users).** Your IT administrator may not have enabled Copilot for your account or department. Contact your IT team. 5. **Platform.** Copilot in Microsoft 365 apps runs on Windows, Mac, web, and mobile, but feature availability varies by platform.

Copilot Cannot Access My Files or Data

The problem: You asked Copilot about a document or email, and it says it cannot find it.

Check the following: - **Are the files in OneDrive or SharePoint?** Copilot only reaches files stored in Microsoft's cloud, not files on your local hard drive. - **Do you have permission?** Copilot can only see files you have permission to view. If the file lives in a SharePoint site you do not belong to, Copilot cannot reach it. - **Is the file type supported?** Copilot handles common types (Word, Excel, PowerPoint, PDF) but not every format. - **Is Microsoft Graph connected?** Organizational data access requires your account to be properly connected to Microsoft Graph. Contact IT if you suspect a configuration issue.

Image Generation Is Not Working

The problem: Copilot will not generate images, or you have run out of image generation credits.

Check the following: - **Credits.** Image generation uses "boosts" (credits). Free users get a limited number; paid users get more. If you are out, wait for them to refresh or upgrade your plan. - **Content restrictions.** Copilot will not generate images of real people (by name), violent content, explicit content, or anything that violates Microsoft's usage policies. - **Specificity.** If the images miss your intent, be more descriptive. Include style, colors, composition, and mood.

Copilot Is Slow

The problem: Responses are taking a long time to generate.

Possible causes: - **Think Deeper mode.** Extended reasoning takes longer by design. If you are using Think Deeper for a simple question, switch to Quick Response or Auto. - **Server load.** Peak times slow responses. This is temporary. - **Complex prompts.** Very long prompts with extensive context take longer to process. - **Internet connection.** A slow connection delays the display of responses.

Copilot in Edge Is Not Showing

The problem: The Copilot sidebar is not appearing in Microsoft Edge.

Check the following: 1. Update Edge to the latest version. 2. Click the Copilot icon in the toolbar (top right) or use Ctrl + Shift + . (period). 3. Check that Copilot is not disabled in Edge settings (Settings > Sidebar > Copilot). 4. If you are using Edge at work, your organization may have disabled the Copilot sidebar. 5. Restart Edge.

GitHub Copilot Is Not Suggesting Code

The problem: You are typing in your editor but not seeing inline suggestions from GitHub Copilot.

Check the following: 1. **Extension installed?** Verify the GitHub Copilot extension is installed and enabled. 2. **Signed in?** Confirm you are signed in to a GitHub account with an active Copilot subscription. 3. **Subscription active?** Check that your Copilot Free/Pro/Pro+/Business/Enterprise subscription is current. 4. **Language supported?** Copilot works best with popular languages. It is less active in obscure or domain-specific ones. 5. **Settings.** Confirm inline suggestions are enabled (in VS Code: Settings > search "Copilot"). 6. **Network.** GitHub Copilot requires an internet connection. It does not work offline.

Copilot Gives Different Answers to the Same Question

The problem: You asked the same question twice and got two different responses.

This is normal. AI models have an element of randomness (called "temperature") in their generation. Responses vary even for identical prompts. If you need consistency: - Copy and save responses you want to reference later. - Use specific prompts with tighter constraints to reduce variation. - In some enterprise configurations, temperature and other parameters are adjustable.

Copilot's Formatting Is Messy When I Paste

The problem: When you copy Copilot's response and paste it elsewhere, the formatting does not look right.

Fixes by destination: - **Word/Google Docs:** Use "Paste and Match Formatting" (Ctrl + Shift + V) to strip Markdown and match your document's style. - **Email:** Most clients handle pasted formatted text well. If not, paste as plain text and reformat. - **Spreadsheets:** For table data, paste into a plain text editor first, then into your spreadsheet. - **Plain text editors:** Copilot's output includes Markdown characters (#, , |). **They will not render in plain text — that is expected. -** Use Copilot in the app directly.** The best formatting experience comes from running Copilot inside Microsoft 365 apps, where output is automatically styled for the host application.

General Troubleshooting Steps

When all else fails, try these in order:

1. **Refresh the page or restart the app.**
2. **Clear your browser cache** (if using web Copilot).
3. **Sign out and sign back in** to your Microsoft account.
4. **Check the Microsoft 365 Service Health page** for outages.
5. **Try a different browser or device** to isolate the issue.
6. **Check the Microsoft Copilot support page** at support.microsoft.com for known issues and updates.
7. **Contact support.** Microsoft 365 business and enterprise customers can reach Microsoft support directly. Consumers can use the Microsoft support community.

Appendix D: Glossary of AI Terms

This glossary covers the most important terms you will encounter when using Microsoft Copilot and reading about AI. Definitions are written in plain language — no computer science degree required.

Agent / Agentic AI. An AI system that can take actions on your behalf, not just generate text. Agentic AI can browse the web, execute code, interact with apps, and complete multi-step tasks autonomously. Copilot's agent capabilities are expanding rapidly.

AI (Artificial Intelligence). A broad term for computer systems that can perform tasks that normally require human intelligence — understanding language, recognizing patterns, making decisions, and generating content.

Alignment. The process of training an AI model to behave in ways that are helpful, honest, and safe — aligned with human values and intentions. Alignment is one of the biggest challenges in AI development.

Bias. Systematic errors in AI output that reflect imbalances in training data or design choices. For example, an AI might associate certain professions with specific genders because its training data did. See Chapter 25.

Bing Search Grounding. Copilot's ability to search the web through Bing to provide current, cited information. This helps Copilot answer questions about recent events and reduces hallucination for factual queries.

Chatbot. A software program designed to have conversations with humans. Copilot is a chatbot, but the term undersells its capabilities — it is more accurately described as an AI assistant.

Commercial Data Protection (CDP). Microsoft's guarantee that data from business and enterprise Copilot users is not used to train AI models. This is a key privacy feature for organizational deployments.

Completion. In AI, a completion is the text generated by a model in response to a prompt. When you ask Copilot a question, the answer is the completion.

Context Window. The total amount of text (measured in tokens) that a language model can process at once. This includes both your input and the model's response. Larger context windows allow for longer conversations and larger document analysis.

Copilot Pages. A collaborative canvas within Microsoft Copilot where you can save, edit, and share AI-generated content. Pages allow multiple people to work with and refine Copilot's output together.

Copilot Studio. Microsoft's platform for creating custom Copilot agents and plugins. Organizations can use Copilot Studio to build AI-powered workflows tailored to their specific needs.

DALL-E. An earlier OpenAI image generation model family. Copilot's image generation has transitioned to GPT Image 1.5 (rolling out since January 2026); DALL-E 3 is being deprecated in May 2026.

GPT Image 1.5. OpenAI's current image generation model, the successor to DALL-E 3. Copilot began rolling it out as the backend for Copilot image generation in January 2026.

Deep Learning. A subset of machine learning that uses neural networks with many layers to learn complex patterns. The large language models powering Copilot are products of deep learning.

Designer (Microsoft). Microsoft's AI-powered image creation and design tool, integrated into Copilot for image generation.

Embedding. A mathematical representation of text (or images, or other data) that captures its meaning. Embeddings allow AI systems to find and compare similar content. Microsoft Graph uses embeddings to help Copilot find relevant documents in your organization.

Enterprise Data Protection. Extended data governance features available in Microsoft 365 Copilot Enterprise, including eDiscovery, advanced compliance, and custom data residency controls.

Few-Shot Prompting. A prompting technique where you provide the AI with a few examples of the input-output pattern you want before asking it to perform the task. "Here are three examples of good product descriptions. Now write one for this product."

Fine-Tuning. The process of further training a pre-trained model on a specific dataset to improve its performance for a particular task or domain. In GitHub Copilot Enterprise, models can be fine-tuned on an organization's codebase.

Foundation Model. A large AI model trained on broad data that can be adapted to many tasks. GPT-5.4, Claude, and Gemini are all foundation models.

Generative AI (GenAI). AI systems that create new content — text, images, code, music, video — rather than just analyzing or classifying existing content. Copilot is a generative AI tool.

GPT (Generative Pre-trained Transformer). The family of language models created by OpenAI that power many of Copilot's capabilities. GPT-5.4 is the current frontier model.

Grounding. The process of connecting AI responses to real-world data sources to improve accuracy. Copilot uses Bing Search grounding (web data) and Microsoft Graph grounding (organizational data).

Guardrails. Safety measures built into AI systems to prevent harmful, inappropriate, or dangerous outputs. Copilot has content filters, safety protocols, and behavioral guidelines that act as guardrails.

Hallucination. When an AI generates information that sounds plausible but is factually incorrect or completely fabricated. See Chapter 25 for detailed coverage.

Inference. The process of running a trained AI model to generate responses. When you send a prompt to Copilot, the inference happens on Microsoft's servers.

Large Language Model (LLM). An AI model trained on massive amounts of text data that can understand and generate human language. GPT-5.4, Claude, and Gemini are all large language models.

Machine Learning (ML). A branch of AI where systems learn from data and improve through experience, rather than being explicitly programmed for every task.

Microsoft 365 Copilot. The AI assistant integrated into Microsoft 365 applications (Word, Excel, PowerPoint, Outlook, Teams). Available in Business and Enterprise tiers.

Microsoft 365 Graph. Microsoft's data layer that connects all your Microsoft 365 data — emails, documents, calendar, contacts, Teams chats, and more. Copilot for Business uses Microsoft 365 Graph to access organizational data.

Model. In AI, a model is the trained system that processes inputs and generates outputs. Different models have different capabilities, strengths, and weaknesses.

Multimodal. An AI system that can process multiple types of input — text, images, audio, video. Copilot is multimodal: it can accept text and images as input.

Natural Language Processing (NLP). The branch of AI focused on enabling computers to understand, interpret, and generate human language.

Neural Network. A computing system inspired by the structure of the human brain, consisting of interconnected nodes (neurons) organized in layers. Neural networks are the foundation of modern AI.

Parameter. A tunable value within a neural network that the model adjusts during training. Larger models have more parameters and generally exhibit more sophisticated behavior. Modern large language models have hundreds of billions or trillions of parameters.

Plugin. An extension that adds new capabilities to Copilot. Plugins can connect Copilot to external services, databases, or specialized tools.

Pre-Training. The initial phase of training a language model, where it learns from a massive dataset of text. Pre-training gives the model its general language understanding and knowledge.

Prompt. The input you give to an AI model — your question, instruction, or request. The quality of your prompt significantly affects the quality of the response. See Chapter 19.

Prompt Engineering. The practice of crafting effective prompts to get the best results from AI models. This includes specifying roles, providing context, defining formats, and setting constraints.

Prompt Injection. A security attack where malicious text embedded in a document or webpage attempts to manipulate the AI's behavior, potentially causing it to ignore its instructions or reveal information it should not.

RAG (Retrieval-Augmented Generation). A technique where the AI retrieves relevant information from a knowledge base before generating a response. This improves accuracy and allows the AI to reference specific, up-to-date information. Copilot uses RAG when it searches Bing or Microsoft Graph data.

Reinforcement Learning from Human Feedback (RLHF). A training technique where human evaluators rate AI responses, and those ratings are used to train the model to produce better outputs. This is how AI models learn to be helpful and safe.

Responsible AI. A framework of principles and practices for developing and deploying AI systems ethically, including fairness, transparency, accountability, and safety. Microsoft has published Responsible AI principles that govern Copilot's development.

Sensitivity Labels. Microsoft Information Protection labels (Confidential, Internal, Public, etc.) that classify documents by sensitivity level. Copilot respects these labels and will not surface restricted content to users without appropriate permissions.

Sycophancy. The tendency of AI models to agree with the user or tell them what they want to hear, rather than providing honest, accurate, or balanced responses. Modern models are trained to reduce sycophancy, but it still occurs.

Temperature. A setting that controls the randomness of an AI model's responses. Higher temperature produces more creative, varied responses. Lower temperature produces more focused, deterministic responses.

Think Deeper. Copilot's extended reasoning mode, which gives the model more time to work through complex problems before responding. Best for multi-step reasoning, analysis, and problems that benefit from careful thought.

Token. The basic unit of text that language models process. A token is roughly equivalent to three-quarters of a word. "Microsoft Copilot is helpful" is approximately five tokens.

Training Data. The dataset used to train an AI model. For large language models, this includes books, websites, articles, code, and other text sources. The training data affects the model's knowledge, capabilities, and biases.

Transformer. The neural network architecture that powers modern large language models. Transformers process text by attending to relationships between all words in a sequence simultaneously, enabling sophisticated language understanding.

Zero-Shot Prompting. Asking an AI to perform a task without providing any examples — just the instruction. "Translate this sentence to French" is a zero-shot prompt. Compare with few-shot prompting, where you provide examples first.

Appendix E: What's New in 2025-2026

Microsoft Copilot has evolved rapidly since its initial launch. A timeline of the major milestones, feature releases, and strategic shifts that have shaped the product covered in this book.

Pre-2025 Highlights

GitHub Copilot Free Tier (December 2024). GitHub introduced a Free tier offering 2,000 code completions and 50 chat messages per month. This dramatically expanded access to AI coding assistance and cemented GitHub Copilot as an essential tool for developers at all levels. (As covered in Chapter 24, GitHub Copilot is moving to usage-based billing with monthly AI Credits beginning June 1, 2026.)

2025 Timeline

Q1 2025 (January - March)

Copilot Vision Preview. Microsoft introduced Copilot Vision as a limited preview, letting Copilot in Edge see and understand what is on your screen. Initial capabilities focused on browser content — answering questions about visible web pages and helping users navigate complex sites. Vision has since gone generally available across Windows, macOS, Edge, iOS, and Android for personal Microsoft accounts (commercial Entra ID accounts excluded).

Think Deeper Launch. Copilot gained extended reasoning through Think Deeper mode, powered by advanced reasoning models. Users could now tackle multi-step problems requiring sustained logic: math, strategic analysis, detailed planning.

Copilot Pages General Availability. After a preview period, Copilot Pages became generally available — a collaborative AI canvas for saving, editing, and sharing Copilot-generated content. Pages bridged the gap between disposable chat responses and persistent, editable documents.

Microsoft 365 Copilot Expansion. Microsoft pushed Copilot into more Microsoft 365 applications, including deeper integration with OneNote, Loop, and Planner. The goal: make Copilot available wherever Microsoft 365 users work, not just in the core Office apps.

Q2 2025 (April - June)

Copilot Studio Enhancements. Microsoft expanded Copilot Studio, the platform for building custom Copilot agents. New features: more sophisticated workflow automation, better third-party data source integration, and improved no-code/low-code building. Organizations could now build AI agents tailored to specific business processes.

GitHub Copilot Multi-Model Support. GitHub Copilot introduced multi-model support, letting developers choose between different AI models (initially GPT and Claude) for code completion and chat. A significant strategic shift — an acknowledgment that different models excel at different tasks.

Copilot for Mobile Improvements. The Copilot mobile app received major updates: better voice conversations, tighter camera integration for visual analysis, and a more intuitive interface for on-the-go productivity.

Enterprise Analytics Dashboard. Microsoft launched enhanced analytics for Microsoft 365 Copilot administrators, surfacing adoption rates, common use cases, and productivity impact across the organization.

Q3 2025 (July - September)

GPT-5 Release and Integration. OpenAI released GPT-5 in August 2025, and Microsoft began rolling out GPT-5-powered experiences across Copilot products soon after. The upgrade brought improved instruction following, better factual accuracy, and more natural conversation.

Agentic Capabilities Expansion. Copilot grew more autonomous, moving beyond simple Q&A toward completing multi-step tasks with minimal user intervention. Early agentic features included automated email triage, meeting scheduling, and document workflow management.

Copilot in Teams Enhancements. Teams Copilot started participating more actively in meetings — offering real-time summaries, suggesting follow-up questions, and drafting action items as conversations unfolded, not only after they ended.

Microsoft 365 Copilot Price Restructuring. Microsoft adjusted its Microsoft 365 Copilot licensing, introducing more flexible pricing to accelerate enterprise adoption. The changes opened Copilot to a broader range of organization sizes and budgets.

Q4 2025 (October - December)

GPT-5.2 Rollout (December 2025). OpenAI's GPT-5.2 model began powering Copilot experiences, with gains in coding, reasoning, and lower hallucination rates compared to the initial GPT-5 release. Microsoft 365 Copilot picked it up on December 15, 2025.

Copilot Vision Expansion. Copilot Vision moved beyond browser-only use, gaining the ability to read content from more applications and screen contexts. Privacy controls were refined to give users granular control over what Copilot could see.

GitHub Copilot Pro+ Launch. GitHub introduced the Pro+ tier at $39/month, offering frontier models with higher rate limits, advanced agent capabilities, and pull request summaries. This drew a clearer line between individual and professional developer needs.

Gemini Model Added to GitHub Copilot. GitHub Copilot extended multi-model support to include Google's Gemini, giving developers three major model families: GPT, Claude, and Gemini.

Year-End Adoption Milestones. Microsoft reported that Microsoft 365 Copilot had reached significant adoption across Fortune 500 companies, with measurable productivity gains. GitHub Copilot crossed major thresholds in developer adoption worldwide.

Q1 2026 (January - March)

GPT Image 1.5 Rollout. OpenAI's GPT Image 1.5 — the successor to DALL-E 3 — began rolling out as the backend for Copilot's image generation in January 2026. (DALL-E 3 itself is being deprecated in May 2026.)

Conversation Modes Refinement. Copilot streamlined its conversation modes to three clear options: Quick Response (fast, concise answers), Auto (intelligent mode selection), and Think Deeper (extended reasoning for complex problems). This replaced earlier, less intuitive naming.

GPT-5.4 Thinking in Copilot (March 2026). OpenAI's GPT-5.4 Thinking model rolled into Microsoft 365 Copilot on March 6, 2026, becoming the model behind Think Deeper. A significant leap in complex reasoning, coding, and creative tasks.

Enhanced Privacy Controls. Microsoft introduced more granular privacy controls across all Copilot tiers, including clearer opt-out mechanisms for data usage and better transparency about how conversations are processed and stored.

Copilot in Education. Microsoft rolled out education-specific Copilot features: integration with Microsoft 365 Education plans, age-appropriate content controls, and tools built for classroom use. Institutions gained tighter administrative control over student AI access.

GitHub Copilot Tier Consolidation. The five GitHub Copilot tiers (Free, Pro, Pro+, Business, Enterprise) were clarified and stabilized, with sharper feature differentiation and more flexible enterprise licensing.

Performance and Reliability Improvements. Across all Copilot products, Microsoft focused on speed, reliability, and consistency. Response times improved, especially for Think Deeper mode, and uptime targets rose for enterprise customers.

Q2 2026 (April - May, partial)

GPT-5.5 Thinking on Selected Surfaces. Microsoft began adding the newer GPT-5.5 Thinking model to some Copilot surfaces for even deeper reasoning, alongside the existing GPT-5.4 Thinking option.

DALL-E 3 Deprecation. Microsoft's image generation pipeline completed the transition off DALL-E 3 (formally deprecated May 12, 2026) and onto GPT Image 1.5.

GitHub Copilot Billing Transition. Beginning June 1, 2026, all GitHub Copilot plans transition to usage-based billing with monthly AI Credits, replacing the prior fixed completion and chat allowances.

Looking Ahead

The pace of change in AI shows no signs of slowing. As this book goes to press, several developments are on the horizon:

- **Deeper agentic capabilities.** Copilot is moving toward more autonomous task completion — handling complex, multi-step workflows with less manual intervention.
- **Improved personalization.** Copilot is learning to adapt to individual users' preferences, communication styles, and work patterns over time.
- **Broader multi-modal support.** Video understanding, richer image analysis, and more capable audio interactions are in development.
- **Tighter Microsoft ecosystem integration.** Expect Copilot in more Microsoft products and tighter coordination across the Microsoft 365 ecosystem.
- **New model capabilities.** As foundation models advance, Copilot's underlying capabilities will improve in reasoning, factual accuracy, and nuanced language understanding.

The features described in this book reflect Copilot as of May 2026. For the latest updates, visit the Microsoft Copilot blog (blogs.microsoft.com/copilot) and the GitHub Copilot changelog (github.blog).

Appendix F: Resources and Further Reading

The most useful resources for continuing your Copilot journey beyond this book, organized by category, with brief descriptions to help you find what you need.

Official Microsoft Resources

Microsoft Copilot - Copilot web app: copilot.microsoft.com - Copilot blog: blogs.microsoft.com/copilot - Copilot support: support.microsoft.com (search "Copilot")

Microsoft 365 Copilot (Business and Enterprise) - Adoption hub: adoption.microsoft.com/copilot - Admin documentation: learn.microsoft.com/copilot - Microsoft 365 Copilot plans and pricing: microsoft.com/microsoft-365/copilot

GitHub Copilot - GitHub Copilot home: github.com/features/copilot - GitHub Copilot documentation: docs.github.com/copilot - GitHub blog (Copilot updates): github.blog - GitHub Copilot pricing: github.com/features/copilot/plans

Microsoft Learn - Free training modules on Copilot: learn.microsoft.com (search "Copilot") - Microsoft 365 Copilot learning paths for end users, administrators, and developers

Copilot Studio - Documentation: learn.microsoft.com/copilot-studio - For building custom Copilot agents and plugins

---

The AI for Everyone Series from Finnoybu Press

This book is part of the **AI for Everyone** series by Finnoybu Press, designed to help real people use AI tools effectively. Every title follows the same practical, authoritative style as this one.

Collection 1: Core Tools

- **ChatGPT: The Definitive Guide (2026 Edition)** – A complete guide to OpenAI's ChatGPT, covering Free through Enterprise tiers, GPT-5.x models, Agent Mode, Deep Research, DALL-E image generation, Sora video, voice mode, Custom GPTs, and the full ChatGPT ecosystem.
- **ChatGPT: The Power User Guide (2026 Edition)** – Advanced techniques for experienced ChatGPT users: prompt architecture, chain-of-thought reasoning, multi-turn mastery, reusable prompt systems, advanced content production, API integration, and building professional workflows.
- **Claude: The Definitive Guide (2026 Edition)** – A comprehensive guide to Anthropic's Claude, covering all tiers and models, Projects, Artifacts, extended thinking, vision, writing, coding, and Claude's distinctive approach to safety and reasoning.
- **Claude Code: The Power User Guide (2026 Edition)** – The definitive guide to Claude Code, Anthropic's agentic coding tool. Covers installation, code generation, debugging, testing, multi-file operations, Git workflows, hooks, MCP servers, IDE integrations, and team workflows.

Collection 2: Essential Platforms

- **Gemini: The Complete Guide (2026 Edition)** – A complete guide to Google's Gemini, including Gemini in Google Workspace, Gemini Advanced, AI Studio, multimodal capabilities, and the Google AI ecosystem.
- **Gemini: The Advanced Guide (2026 Edition)** – Advanced Gemini techniques for power users across Google's AI ecosystem.
- **Microsoft Copilot: The Workplace AI Guide (2026 Edition)** – *This book*. A complete guide to Microsoft Copilot across the entire Microsoft ecosystem.
- **Microsoft Copilot: The Advanced Workplace Guide (2026 Edition)** – Advanced companion to this book, covering Copilot Studio, custom agents, Power Automate integration, enterprise deployment, and developer workflows.
- **Perplexity AI: The Research Playbook (2026 Edition)** – A practical guide to Perplexity AI for research, discovery, and information synthesis.

- **Perplexity AI: The Advanced Research Playbook (2026 Edition)** — Advanced Perplexity techniques for professional research workflows.

Collection 3: Authoritative Series

- **AI Systems Playbook (2026 Edition)** — A strategic guide to evaluating, selecting, and deploying AI tools across an organization.
- **AI Prompt Engineering (2026 Edition)** — A deep dive into prompt engineering techniques that work across all major AI platforms.
- **AI for Developers (2026 Edition)** — A practical guide to integrating AI into software development workflows, from coding assistants to CI/CD pipelines.
- **AI for Business (2026 Edition)** — A practical guide to AI-powered productivity for professionals, teams, and organizations.
- **AI for Students (2026 Edition)** — A guide to using AI tools responsibly and effectively in academic work.

All titles available at press.finnoybu.org. For publisher inquiries: press@finnoybu.org.

AI News and Analysis

The Verge — AI Section theverge.com/ai-artificial-intelligence Accessible, well-reported coverage of AI developments and products.

Ars Technica — AI Section arstechnica.com/ai In-depth technical coverage with excellent analysis.

MIT Technology Review — AI technologyreview.com/artificial-intelligence Thoughtful long-form journalism on AI's impact and trajectory.

Ben Thompson's Stratechery stratechery.com Paid newsletter with excellent strategic analysis of technology companies and AI trends.

One Useful Thing (Ethan Mollick) oneusefulthing.org A Wharton professor writing practically and thoughtfully about AI's impact on work and education. Highly recommended.

AI Ethics and Safety

Partnership on AI partnershiponai.org Multi-stakeholder organization focused on responsible AI development and deployment.

AI Now Institute ainowinstitute.org Research institute focused on the social implications of AI.

Microsoft Responsible AI microsoft.com/ai/responsible-ai Microsoft's responsible AI principles and practices.

Stanford HAI (Human-Centered Artificial Intelligence) hai.stanford.edu Academic research and policy work on AI's impact on society.

Learning Resources

Microsoft Learn — AI Skills learn.microsoft.com Free, structured learning paths for Copilot and other Microsoft AI tools. Hands-on exercises and certifications included.

LinkedIn Learning linkedin.com/learning Video courses on Microsoft Copilot, Microsoft 365, and AI productivity. Many are updated regularly.

YouTube — Microsoft Mechanics Channel youtube.com/@MSFTMechanics Official Microsoft channel with demos and explainers for Copilot features.

YouTube — Microsoft 365 Community Product demos, tips, and how-to videos from Microsoft and community creators.

Communities

Microsoft Tech Community — Copilot techcommunity.microsoft.com Official community forums for Microsoft Copilot discussions, questions, and feature requests.

Reddit — r/MicrosoftCopilot Community discussions, tips, and experiences with Microsoft Copilot.

Reddit — r/github (GitHub Copilot discussions) Developer community discussions about GitHub Copilot.

GitHub Community Discussions github.community Official GitHub community for GitHub Copilot and other GitHub products.

Prompt Engineering

Microsoft Copilot Lab copilot.cloud.microsoft/prompts Microsoft's official prompt gallery with categorized examples for Copilot in Microsoft 365 apps.

Learn Prompting learnprompting.org Free, open-source guide to prompt engineering. Not Copilot-specific, but the techniques apply broadly.

Anthropic's Prompt Engineering Guide docs.anthropic.com/claude/docs/prompt-engineering Excellent guide to prompt engineering from the makers of Claude. Many techniques transfer to Copilot.

For Developers

GitHub Copilot Documentation docs.github.com/copilot Official documentation covering setup, features, best practices, and troubleshooting.

VS Code Documentation — Copilot code.visualstudio.com/docs/copilot Documentation specific to using Copilot in Visual Studio Code.

GitHub Copilot Trust Center github.com/features/copilot/trust Security, privacy, and IP information for GitHub Copilot.

For IT Administrators

Microsoft 365 Copilot Deployment Guide learn.microsoft.com/copilot/microsoft-365/microsoft-365-copilot-setup Step-by-step deployment guidance for rolling out Copilot in an organization.

Microsoft Purview Compliance learn.microsoft.com/purview Data governance and compliance tools that integrate with Copilot.

Microsoft Entra ID (Identity Management) learn.microsoft.com/entra Identity and access management for controlling Copilot access in organizations.

Books

Co-Intelligence: Living and Working with AI by Ethan Mollick (2024) An accessible, practical book on working with AI effectively, by the Wharton professor behind the One Useful Thing newsletter.

The AI-Powered Workplace (various authors, 2025-2026) Multiple titles on AI in professional settings. Check your preferred bookseller for current options.

Resources and URLs were verified as of May 2026. In a fast-moving landscape, specific URLs may change. When in doubt, search the site name directly.

www.ingramcontent.com/pod-product-compliance
Lightning Source LLC
LaVergne TN
LVHW060027210926
848481LV00013B/3802
9798950533068